THE
DAWN OF
CHRISTIANITY

A History of the First Century Church

MICHAEL LEE

TABLE OF CONTENTS

DEDICATION

This book is dedicated to all who seek to understand the roots of their faith, the history of Christianity, and the enduring power of its message. May this exploration of the early church illuminate the path toward a deeper appreciation for the foundations of a transformative faith that continues to shape the world today.

And especially to my God-Fearing wife and best friend, Laura

PREFACE

Few events in the tapestry of human history have left a mark as profound and enduring as the rise of Christianity. From its humble beginnings in the turbulent world of first-century Palestine, this faith spread across the Roman Empire and beyond, transforming cultures, shaping societies, and influencing the course of civilization.

This book embarks on a journey through the vibrant and dynamic early years of Christianity, offering a glimpse into the lives, beliefs, and challenges of those who laid the foundation for a faith that continues to inspire and guide billions worldwide.

We will delve into the historical context of Jesus' ministry, examining the social, political, and religious influences that shaped his teachings and the nascent Christian movement. We will trace the journeys of the apostles and disciples as they spread the Gospel message, encountering both acceptance and persecution and establishing churches in diverse regions. We will explore the development of Christian theology and doctrine, the emergence of early church leaders, and the rise of monasticism, which has profoundly influenced the spiritual landscape of the ancient world.

This book aims to illuminate the complexities of this transformative period, providing insights into the historical context, cultural influences, and theological debates that shaped the early church. We hope to offer a compelling and enriching exploration of Christianity's origins and formative years by weaving together historical facts, theological reflections, and captivating narratives.

INTRODUCTION

The story of early Christianity is a tale of fragility and resilience, persecution and triumph, division and unity. It is a narrative of individuals who dared to believe in a radical message of love, forgiveness, and hope, faced extraordinary challenges to spread their faith, and left a legacy that continues to inspire and shape societies across the globe.

To comprehend the origins and evolution of this transformative faith, we must embark on a journey back to the tumultuous world of first-century Palestine, a land steeped in history and cultural complexity. Here, amidst the backdrop of Roman rule, Jewish tradition, and the burgeoning influence of Hellenistic thought, Jesus of Nazareth emerged, proclaiming a message that would ignite a movement unlike the world had ever seen.

This book will guide us through the formative years of Christianity, tracing the evolution of the faith from the time of Jesus' ministry through the establishment of early churches and the spread of the Gospel message to diverse regions. We will explore the lives and legacies of prominent early church figures, shedding light on their pivotal roles in shaping the nascent Christian community.

We will examine the challenges faced by early Christians, including Roman persecution, societal opposition, and internal disputes within the emerging church. We will also delve into the development of Christian theology and doctrine, the emergence of monasticism, and the enduring legacy of the Church Fathers, whose writings and teachings continue to influence Christian thought and practice today.

This exploration of early Christianity is a historical exercise and a journey into the heart of a faith that has shaped human history. By understanding the origins and formative years of Christianity, we gain a deeper appreciation for its enduring power, its diverse expressions, and its ongoing relevance in the world today.

1.   THE HISTORICAL CONTEXT OF JESUS' MINISTRY

The ministry of Jesus unfolded against the backdrop of a tumultuous first-century Palestine, a land caught in the crosshairs of mighty empires and fraught with social and religious tensions. At its zenith, the Roman Empire cast a long shadow over the region, wielding its military might and imposing its laws on Judea and its surrounding territories. The Jewish people, yearning for independence and struggling under Roman rule, were divided in their response to the occupying force. Some sought peaceful resistance through adherence to the Law and the teachings of the prophets, while others embraced revolutionary movements hoping to overthrow Roman dominance.

This political backdrop was further complicated by the complex social fabric of the time. Jewish society was highly stratified, with a powerful priestly elite, wealthy landowners, and merchants alongside a vast population of poor and marginalized individuals. The gap between rich and poor was stark, and poverty was a pervasive reality for many. The social system was characterized by strict gender roles, with women primarily relegated to the domestic sphere.

Alongside these social divisions, a vibrant religious landscape existed in first-century Palestine. The Jewish people adhered to the Law of Moses, which has a complex system of rituals, sacrifices, and dietary regulations.

Synagogues, becoming increasingly important centers of Jewish religious life, provided a forum for studying and discussing scripture and practicing communal prayer. However, various religious factions existed within Judaism, each with its own interpretation of the Law and its approach to achieving salvation.

The Pharisees, known for their strict adherence to the Law and their interpretation of tradition, held significant influence. The Sadducees, primarily composed of members of the priestly aristocracy, emphasized the literal interpretation of the Torah and rejected the concept of resurrection. The Essenes, a sect that withdrew from society to live a communal life in the desert, focused on purity and awaited the coming of a righteous Messiah. The Zealots, driven by a fervent passion for Jewish independence, were prepared to use violence to achieve their goals.

Amidst this intricate tapestry of political, social, and religious currents, Jesus emerged. His teachings, which emphasized love, compassion, and the importance of a personal relationship with God, resonated with many, particularly those who felt marginalized and oppressed. He challenged the authority of the religious establishment, denouncing hypocrisy and advocating for a radical reinterpretation of the Law.

Jesus' message was deeply rooted in the Jewish tradition. Yet, it offered a fresh and revolutionary perspective on the nature of God, the path to salvation, and the meaning of true discipleship. His parables, short stories filled with vivid imagery and profound insights, offered a powerful way to communicate his teachings and challenge his listeners' assumptions. He used simple metaphors, drawing from everyday life and natural phenomena, to illustrate complex spiritual truths. His teachings on the importance of forgiveness, true love, and the call to a life of service were revolutionary and deeply resonant with the human spirit.

One of the central themes of Jesus' ministry was the coming of the Kingdom of God, a concept he presented as a realm of peace, justice, and righteousness. He declared that the Kingdom was "at hand," meaning it was both present and future, a reality that could be experienced in the present through his teachings and his actions. This message of hope and transformation resonated deeply with those who felt oppressed by Roman rule and yearning for a better world.

Mighty miracles and profound teachings marked Jesus' life. He healed the sick, calmed storms, and even raised the dead, demonstrating the power of God's grace and authority as the Son of God. These miraculous signs, alongside his teachings, attracted large crowds and drew attention from religious leaders and Roman officials.

Jesus' ministry was not without controversy. His teachings and healing miracles challenged the religious authorities, earning the ire of the Pharisees and Sadducees, who saw him as a threat to their authority. His message of radical love and forgiveness was seen as a direct challenge to the prevailing social order based on rigid hierarchies and strict boundaries. He also attracted the attention of Roman officials, who viewed his growing popularity with suspicion, fearing that he might threaten their control.

The historical context of Jesus' ministry, with its political turmoil, social inequalities, and diverse religious factions, shaped his teachings and provided fertile ground for the emergence of a new movement. His message of love, forgiveness, and the coming of the Kingdom of God resonated deeply with those who felt marginalized and oppressed, offering a path to hope and transformation. His life, teachings, and ultimate sacrifice on the cross laid the foundation for the burgeoning Christian faith, spreading rapidly throughout Rome and beyond, profoundly transforming the world and influencing history.

2. JESUS' LIFE TEACHINGS AND IMPACT

Jesus, a Jewish teacher from Nazareth in Galilee, emerged as a pivotal figure in the first century, captivating hearts and minds with his profound teachings and life of compassion. His ministry, rooted in the Jewish tradition, challenged existing religious and social norms, offering a transformative vision of God's love and the kingdom of heaven. His message resonated with the marginalized and oppressed, challenging the established power structures of his time.

Jesus' life was marked by a profound connection with God, evident in his miracles, teachings, and unwavering commitment to service. He healed the sick, calmed storms, and fed the hungry, demonstrating God's power and love through tangible acts. His parables, stories that conveyed spiritual truths in relatable terms, challenged listeners to examine their lives and embrace God's grace. The parable of the Good Samaritan, for instance, highlighted the universality of love and compassion, urging people to extend kindness even to those outside their social circles.

Jesus' central message revolved around the kingdom of God, a spiritual reality that transcended earthly boundaries and offered a new perspective on life and salvation. He emphasized forgiveness, humility, and the importance of loving one's neighbor as oneself. His teachings challenged the rigid legalism of his time, focusing on the importance of inner transformation and genuine faith rather than outward observance of religious rituals. His call to "love your enemies" and "turn the other cheek" challenged the prevailing ethos of revenge and violence, offering a radical alternative rooted in forgiveness and peacemaking.

The most significant event in Jesus' life was his crucifixion, a brutal act of violence that many believed marked the ultimate triumph of evil. However, his followers experienced a profound transformation with the resurrection, a pivotal event that transformed their grief into hope and propelled the spread of Christianity. The belief in Jesus' resurrection formed the cornerstone of the Christian faith, offering the promise of eternal life and victory over death.

The impact of Jesus' life, teachings, and resurrection was profound and enduring. His message resonated with diverse audiences, transcending cultural and social boundaries. The early Christian community, rooted in his teachings and empowered by his example, began to spread the Gospel message throughout the Roman Empire. Their unwavering belief in Jesus' message and their commitment to living lives of love and service laid the foundation for the growth of Christianity, which eventually became a dominant force in the Roman world.

Jesus' teachings and example became the foundation for a new spiritual movement that emphasized a personal relationship with God, forgiveness, compassion, and the pursuit of justice. His life and teachings inspire and challenge people across cultures and generations, offering a vision of hope, love, and a transformed world.

3.   THE EARLY DISCIPLES AND THE SPREAD OF THE GOSPEL

The Gospel, meaning "good news," began its journey in the heart of Jerusalem, radiating outward from the disciples of Jesus. They, initially a small band of fishermen and tax collectors, transformed into fervent preachers, carrying the message of Jesus' life, death, and resurrection to their fellow Jews. The story of their mission is an engaging tapestry woven with encounters with diverse individuals and their struggles within Jewish communities.

Imagine the scene: a bustling marketplace in Jerusalem, where people from all walks of life come to buy and sell. The disciples, filled with the Holy Spirit, begin to preach among the crowds, their voices echoing Jesus' words. They speak of Jesus' miracles, teachings, and powerful messages of love and forgiveness. The message resonates with some, stirring their hearts with newfound hope. Others, however, are skeptical and resistant to the radical claims of this new movement.

Peter, known for his boldness and fiery spirit, often found himself at the center of these initial encounters. He delivered powerful sermons, boldly proclaiming Jesus as the Messiah, the promised king of Israel. His words stirred awe and opposition, sparking heated debates within the synagogues and public squares. Yet, through it all, Peter remained steadfast, his conviction unyielding, fueled by his unwavering belief in Jesus' resurrection.

The disciples were not alone in spreading the Gospel. Others, moved by the power of Jesus' message, joined them. One such figure was Philip, known for his gentle nature and deep spiritual understanding. He was instrumental in carrying the Gospel to Samaria, a region often viewed with suspicion by

Jews. Philip's interactions with Samaritans demonstrated that Jesus' message transcended ethnic and religious barriers, reaching out to all open to hearing it.

Another compelling narrative unfolds with the story of Stephen, a man of great faith and eloquent speech. He boldly defended the teachings of Jesus before the Jewish Sanhedrin, the highest religious court. Stephen's powerful defense, however, met with fierce opposition, and he was ultimately stoned to death. His martyrdom, a testament to his unwavering faith, catalyzed the spread of the Gospel, igniting a fervor among the early Christians.

The disciples' journeys were only sometimes smooth sailing. They faced opposition from both Jewish authorities and Roman officials, who viewed Christianity as a subversive force. Their encounters with Roman soldiers, their imprisonment, and their frequent trials underscored the risks they faced, yet they persisted, driven by an unshakeable belief in Jesus' message.

One of the most significant encounters in the early spread of the Gospel involved a Jewish man named Saul of Tarsus, a fierce opponent of Christianity. Saul, consumed by his zeal to stamp out the new religion, was on a mission to persecute Christians in Damascus. However, his journey was interrupted by a dazzling light from heaven and a voice that called out to him, "Saul, Saul, why are you persecuting me?" This life-altering event, later known as Saul's conversion, transformed him into Paul, one of the most influential figures in the early church.

Paul, a man of exceptional intelligence and eloquence, dedicated his life to spreading the Gospel message. He embarked on extensive missionary journeys, traveling throughout the Roman Empire and establishing churches in key cities like Antioch, Ephesus, and Corinth. Paul's encounters with Gentile communities, those who were not Jewish, led him to argue that the Gospel message was not just for the Jews but for all people. He stressed that salvation was available to all who accepted Jesus Christ as Lord and Savior.

Paul's mission, often fraught with challenges, was marked by consequential debates, powerful sermons, and a deep commitment to spreading the Gospel. His letters, later collected in the New Testament, provided invaluable guidance and theological insights to early Christians, shaping the development of Christian thought and practice.

The early disciples and their tireless mission, fueled by the transformative power of the Gospel message, set the stage for the rapid growth of Christianity. Their journey, marked by both persecution and triumph, demonstrates the profound impact of their faith. Their courage, unwavering faith, and deep commitment to carrying Jesus' message to all corners of the world laid the foundation for a faith that would continue to grow and spread, ultimately becoming one of the world's most influential religions.

As we delve deeper into the history of early Christianity, we'll uncover the stories of many other individuals who played pivotal roles in shaping the course of this fledgling religion. Their contributions, encounters, and struggles provide a rich and nuanced understanding of Christianity's origins and development. This faith continues to inspire and shape the world today.

4.   THE DEATH AND RESURRECTION OF JESUS

The death of Jesus on the cross, a brutal and agonizing event, stands as a central pillar in the Christian narrative. It was a historical and pivotal event that deeply resonated with the disciples and laid the foundation for the burgeoning Christian movement. This event, shrouded in profound sorrow and despair, was followed by the remarkable proclamation of Jesus' resurrection, a claim that initially met with disbelief and skepticism.

The historical accounts surrounding Jesus' death and resurrection are multifaceted, interwoven with theological interpretations and profound religious experiences. Historians and scholars grapple with the veracity and nature of these events, carefully dissecting the Gospels and other early Christian writings to reconstruct a comprehensive understanding.

The Gospels, penned by individuals who were either direct witnesses or close associates of Jesus' disciples, offer vivid accounts of his crucifixion, death, and burial. They detail the anguish of his followers, the Roman authority's involvement, and the somber atmosphere surrounding the event. The narratives vividly portray the emotional toll the crucifixion took on Jesus' disciples, leaving them shattered and disillusioned. The death of their leader, their friend, their Messiah, cast a long shadow over their hopes and aspirations.

Yet, amidst the grief and despair, the Gospels introduce a glimmer of hope – the resurrection. They recount the experiences of individuals who encountered Jesus in his resurrected form, providing firsthand accounts of his physical presence, interactions, and declarations. Often imbued with a sense of awe and wonder, these narratives serve as the cornerstone of the Christian faith

The resurrection of Jesus, a central tenet of Christian theology, is not simply a historical event but a transformative act with profound theological implications. It is a testament to Jesus' divine nature, confirming his authority and offering hope for the future. The resurrection signifies a victory over death, promising eternal life and a renewed relationship with God. For the early Christians, the resurrection of Jesus was not merely a belief but an experience that fueled their faith and empowered them to spread the Gospel message with unwavering conviction.

Jesus' death and resurrection impacted the disciples immediately and transformatively. They were initially paralyzed with fear and disbelief, but their encounters with the resurrected Jesus sparked a renewed sense of purpose and mission. Once a scattered group of individuals, the disciples found their lives and identities redefined through these experiences. They became fearless proclaimers of the Gospel, boldly sharing their testimonies and carrying the message of Jesus' resurrection far and wide.

The disciples' transformation, fueled by their encounters with the resurrected Jesus, reverberated through the burgeoning Christian movement. Their unwavering faith and fervent preaching became the driving force behind the rapid spread of Christianity. The message of Jesus' death and resurrection, hope, redemption, and a promise of eternal life resonated with individuals yearning for spiritual meaning and purpose.

The resurrection, then, serves as a turning point in the history of early Christianity. The catalyst fueled the church's growth, transforming a small group of disciples into a powerful movement that challenged the established religious and social order. It is the bedrock upon which the Christian faith is built, offering a foundation for belief, hope, and eternal life.

While the historicity of Jesus' death and resurrection remains a topic of debate among historians and scholars, there is no denying their immense impact on the development of Christianity. The resurrection became a cornerstone of the faith, shaping Christian theology, spirituality, and the essence of Christian identity. It is an event that transcends historical accounts, permeating Christian thought and practice and shaping the lives of countless individuals across generations.

The impact of Jesus' death and resurrection extended beyond the confines of religious belief, influencing the cultural and social landscape of the Roman Empire. The early Christian communities, driven by their faith and inspired by the promise of eternal life, embraced a radical ethic of love, compassion, and forgiveness. This ethic, grounded in the teachings of Jesus and reinforced by the experience of his resurrection, challenged the Roman world's prevailing social norms and structures.

Early Christians extended their compassion to the marginalized and outcasts, providing care for the sick, offering shelter to the homeless, and advocating for the vulnerable. They established communities rooted in shared faith, mutual support, and a commitment to living out the teachings of Jesus. This radical approach, inspired by the transformative message of Jesus' death and resurrection, played a significant role in shaping the moral and social landscape of the Roman Empire, leaving an enduring legacy that continues to influence societies around the world.

The death and resurrection of Jesus remain a cornerstone of the Christian faith, a pivotal event that continues to inspire and challenge individuals across generations. The historical and theological implications of these events are vast and enduring, shaping not only the development of Christianity but also the course of Western civilization and the world at large. Jesus' death and resurrection is a story of sacrifice, redemption, and hope, resonating with individuals seeking meaning, purpose, and connection in a complex world.

5.   THE EARLY CHRISTIAN COMMUNITY

The death and resurrection of Jesus had a profound impact on his disciples, leaving them in a state of grief and wonder. They believed that Jesus was the Messiah, the promised savior, and his death seemed to contradict their expectations. However, the events that unfolded following his crucifixion—his appearances to his disciples and the accounts of his resurrection—gave them a newfound hope and conviction.

The early Christians in Jerusalem, primarily composed of Jesus' disciples and followers, gathered after his crucifixion. They found solace and strength in their faith and belief in Jesus' resurrection. They continued his teachings, focusing on the message of

salvation through faith in him. The disciples, empowered by the Holy Spirit, began sharing the Gospel message among their Jewish communities.

6.   THE EARLY CHRISTIAN COMMUNITY FACED VARIOUS CHALLENGES.

One significant obstacle was the resistance from Jewish leaders who saw Christianity as a threat to their traditional beliefs and practices. They viewed the followers of Jesus as heretics who challenged the authority of the Temple and the established Jewish religious system. This animosity led to persecution, with early Christians often facing ridicule, imprisonment, and even death.

Another challenge, which added to the complexity of the early Christian experience, arose from the diversity of the early Christian communities. While many were Jewish, others were Gentiles who came from different cultural backgrounds. This diversity presented questions about reconciling Jewish law and practices with accepting Gentiles into the Christian faith. Debates arose concerning circumcision, dietary restrictions, and other issues related to Jewish customs.

The first Christian communities sought to address these challenges through communal living, shared resources, and a strong emphasis on prayer and fellowship. They also began to establish a leadership structure, with apostles like Peter and James playing prominent roles in guiding and teaching the early church.

A sense of unity and shared purpose also marked the early Christian communities. They believed in the power of the Holy Spirit to guide them, providing comfort, strength, and courage in the face of adversity. They embraced Jesus' teachings and saw themselves as a new community, bound together by their faith in him and commitment to spreading the Gospel message.

One of the pivotal figures in the early Christian movement was the apostle, Paul. He was a devout Jewish Pharisee who initially persecuted the early Christians. However, he experienced a dramatic conversion on the road to Damascus, where he encountered the risen Jesus and was transformed into a fervent follower.

Paul's ministry was primarily focused on reaching out to Gentiles. He argued that salvation was available to all, not just to Jews. He traveled extensively throughout the Roman Empire, establishing churches in cities like Antioch, Ephesus, and Corinth. His letters to these churches provide invaluable insights into the early Christian faith and the challenges they faced.

In his writings, Paul emphasized the significance of Christ's death and resurrection as the foundation of the Christian faith. He explained that through Jesus' sacrifice, humanity could be reconciled with God and receive forgiveness for their sins. Paul's theology also highlighted the power of the Holy Spirit, which he believed enabled believers to live lives transformed by faith in Christ.

The apostle Peter was crucial in establishing the church in Jerusalem and other parts of Judea. He was one of Jesus' closest disciples, known for his unwavering faith and boldness. Peter's ministry focused on preaching the Gospel to Jewish communities, emphasizing the fulfillment of the messianic prophecies in Jesus.

Peter's leadership was tested when he confronted accusations from the Jewish authorities. He faced persecution, even imprisonment, but his unwavering faith remained strong. His experiences and leadership contributed significantly to the growth and stability of the early church.

The early Christians faced numerous challenges, including persecution, internal disputes, and adapting to diverse cultures. However, they persevered in their faith, building strong communities based on shared beliefs, communal living, and a deep commitment to spreading the Gospel message. The foundation laid by these early communities paved the way for the growth and influence of Christianity throughout the centuries.

The legacy of the early Christian communities extends far beyond their initial struggles and triumphs. Their stories, beliefs, and practices continue to shape the Christian faith today. They inspire believers across the world, reminding them of the transformative power of faith and the enduring message of hope, love, and redemption that lies at the heart of Christianity.

7.   THE PIVOTAL ROLE OF THE APOSTLES

The twelve Apostles, chosen by Jesus himself, formed the core of the early Christian movement. These men, each with unique backgrounds and personalities, made distinct and significant contributions in spreading the Gospel message and establishing the foundation for the organized Christian church.

Peter, the Rock of the Church:
Simon, later known as Peter, was a fisherman from Galilee who became Jesus' most prominent disciple. He was a bold and outspoken leader, often acting as Jesus' spokesperson. After Jesus' resurrection, Peter emerged as a critical figure in the early church in Jerusalem, preaching boldly and leading the community in prayer and fellowship. He was a driving force in the church's outreach to Jewish and Gentile communities, establishing churches in various regions, including Rome. The early church fathers recognized Peter's leadership role, viewing him as the "first among equals" among the Apostles.

Andrew, the First Follower:
Andrew, Peter's brother, was among the first to follow Jesus, witnessing the transformative impact of Jesus' teachings firsthand. He Andrew spread the Gospel message fervently, traveling widely and establishing churches in various regions. He is mainly remembered for his evangelistic zeal, which brought many to faith in Jesus.

James, the Son of Zebedee:
James, a brother of John, was one of Jesus' closest disciples, often sharing in his ministry. He was a fiery and passionate leader known for his bold

pronouncements and strong convictions. James' ministry focused on establishing churches in various regions, including Judea, where he faced persecution and martyrdom. His life serves as a testament to the unwavering commitment of the early Christians to their faith.

John, the Beloved Disciple:

John, James' brother, was a beloved disciple of Jesus, often called "the disciple whom Jesus loved." He was known for his deep spiritual insight and intimate relationship with Jesus. John witnessed significant events in Jesus' ministry, including the Last. Supper and the crucifixion. After Jesus' ascension, John played a prominent role in the early church, writing the Gospel of John, the Book of Revelation, and three epistles, offering profound insights into Jesus' teachings and the nature of the Christian faith. John's writings remain influential for Christians throughout history, providing spiritual guidance and theological depth.

Philip, the Evangelist:

Originally from Bethsaida, Philip was a profoundly spiritual man who sought to understand Jesus' teachings. He was known for his evangelistic zeal, fervently sharing the Gospel message and attracting many to faith in Jesus. Philip played a crucial role in spreading the Gospel beyond Jewish communities, particularly in Samaria, where he encountered the Ethiopian eunuch and shared the good news with him.

Bartholomew (Nathaniel):

Bartholomew, also known as Nathaniel, was a man of great faith and integrity. He was initially skeptical about Jesus' claims but was convinced after a personal encounter with Jesus, becoming a loyal follower. Bartholomew is believed to have spread the Gospel message in diverse regions, including India, where he is revered as a saint.

Thomas, the Doubting Apostle:

Thomas, also known as Didymus, was a disciple known for his doubting nature. After Jesus' resurrection, Thomas expressed skepticism until he physically encountered Jesus. This story is a testament to the human experience of faith, demonstrating that even doubts can be overcome through personal encounters with God. Thomas' journey reflects the challenges and complexities of faith, reminding Christians that doubt is not always a sign of weakness but rather an opportunity to seek more profound understanding.

Matthew, the Tax Collector:
Originally a tax collector, Matthew left his profession to follow Jesus, demonstrating a profound transformation in his life. His story illustrates the transformative power of faith and the invitation extended to all, regardless of their past, to embrace a life of discipleship.

James, the Son of Alphaeus:
This James, often called "the Less" to distinguish him from James the Son of Zebedee, was a prominent figure in the early church. He is believed to have been a close associate of Jesus and played an essential role in spreading the Gospel message. Although his ministry is not detailed extensively in the Bible, his life serves as a testament to the commitment of the early Apostles to sharing the good news of Jesus' love and redemption.

Simon the Cananean (or The Zealot):
Simon, known as the Cananean or the Zealot, was likely a member of a Jewish political movement advocating for overthrowing Roman rule. His commitment to social justice and his passionate belief in the coming of the Kingdom of God made him an asset to the early Christian movement.

Simon's presence among the Apostles underscores the inclusivity of the Christian message, welcoming individuals from diverse backgrounds and perspectives.

Judas Thaddeus:

Judas Thaddeus, sometimes called Jude or Thaddeus, was a disciple known for his faith and dedication to the Gospel message. He is believed to have traveled widely, spreading the message of Jesus' love and redemption and establishing churches in various regions. His ministry serves as a testament to the commitment of the early Apostles to sharing the good news of Jesus' love and redemption.

Judas Iscariot:

Judas Iscariot, sadly, became the betrayer of Jesus, leading to his arrest and crucifixion. His story is a cautionary tale about the dangers of greed, selfishness, and the consequences of turning away from God. Judas' betrayal, however, did not negate the power of Jesus' sacrifice, for it, ultimately paved the way for salvation for all who believe in him.

8.   THE UNIQUE MINISTRY OF EACH APOSTLE:

Each Apostle, despite their shared commitment to following Jesus, embarked on distinct ministries, reflecting their unique gifts and callings. Peter's bold leadership and evangelistic zeal resonated with the early Jewish communities, while John's deep spiritual insight and compassionate heart drew many to the transformative power of faith. Paul's missionary journeys to various regions, especially to Gentile communities, helped shape the spread of Christianity beyond Jewish communities, establishing churches in diverse cultures and laying the foundation for the global expansion of the Christian faith.

The Apostles: More than Just Spreading the Word: While their primary role was undoubtedly spreading the Gospel message, they also played a critical role in shaping the nascent Christian community. They served as leaders, teachers, and mentors, guiding the disciples in understanding Jesus' teachings and fostering unity and fellowship among the believers. They also played a crucial role in addressing practical needs within the early church, ensuring that the community was equipped to meet the challenges of living out their faith in a hostile environment.

9.   THE LEGACY OF THE APOSTLES:

The lives and ministries of the Apostles continue to inspire and challenge Christians today. Their unwavering commitment to following Jesus, courage in the face of persecution, and dedication to spreading the Gospel message provide a timeless example for those seeking to live authentically. Their story highlights the transformative power of faith, the enduring strength of unity, and the enduring message of God's love and grace.

10. THE STORY OF PAUL

Saul, a man of immense intellect and unwavering devotion to his Jewish faith, was initially a staunch opponent of the nascent Christian movement. Witnessing the execution of Stephen, a devout Christian, and the persecution of early believers only fueled his zeal to eliminate this perceived threat to Judaism. However, a transformative encounter with the risen Christ on the road to Damascus irrevocably altered his life's trajectory. Blinded by a celestial light and overwhelmed by a divine presence, Saul entirely transformed. He who once sought to destroy Christianity now embraced it wholeheartedly, becoming the apostle Paul, a champion of the Gospel message.

Paul's conversion marked a pivotal turning point in the history of Christianity. Embracing the teachings of Jesus with fervent passion, he embarked on a series of missionary journeys that would spread the Christian message far beyond the confines of Jewish communities. His commitment to evangelism knew no bounds, leading him to traverse vast distances, facing dangers and hardships with unwavering determination.

Paul's missionary journeys were not merely geographical expeditions; they were journeys of the soul, driven by a profound desire to share the liberating message of Jesus Christ. He established churches in diverse regions, from Antioch, a melting pot of cultures, to Ephesus, a thriving port city, and Rome, the center of the Roman Empire. He faced opposition and persecution in each place, yet his resolve never wavered. His powerful sermons, filled with scriptural wisdom and eloquent reasoning, captivated audiences, converting many to Christianity.

Paul's writings, preserved in the New Testament as epistles, serve as invaluable windows into his profound theological insights and practical guidance for early Christian communities. His letters to churches in Corinth, Galatia, and Rome, among others, address a wide range of issues, from the nature of faith and salvation to the practicalities of Christian living in a complex society.

One of Paul's most enduring contributions was his ardent belief that the Gospel message was not confined to the Jewish people but was intended for all humanity. This revolutionary idea, known as the "inclusion of the Gentiles," challenged the established norms of his time, opening the doors of Christianity to people of diverse backgrounds and cultures. Paul's efforts to bridge the divide between Judaism and Christianity while navigating complex cultural and theological tensions ultimately led to establishing a genuinely global Christian faith.

Paul's theological writings, particularly his articulation of justification by faith, were instrumental in shaping the understanding of Christian salvation. He emphasized that faith in Jesus Christ, not adherence to Mosaic Law, was the pathway to reconciliation with God. This emphasis on grace, rather than works, offered a liberating message of hope and forgiveness, attracting a wide range of individuals who found solace and purpose in the Christian faith.

Paul's life and ministry exemplified the power of transformation. He went from being a fervent persecutor of Christians to becoming one of Christianity's most influential figures, paving the way for its expansion beyond Jewish communities and into the broader world. His journeys, teachings, and writings inspire and challenge Christians today, offering a profound legacy of faith, courage, and unwavering dedication to the Gospel message.

Paul's missionary journeys were not mere voyages of exploration but epic endeavors propelled by his unwavering faith and an unyielding desire to spread the Gospel message. He faced perils and challenges with steadfast resolve, enduring imprisonment, shipwreck, and even the threat of death. Yet, his commitment to the Christian cause never faltered, and his courage inspired countless others to embrace the message of Jesus Christ.

First Missionary Journey (47-48 CE):

Paul's first missionary journey with Barnabas, his faithful companion, took them from Antioch, where they had been commissioned, to Cyprus, where they encountered Sergius Paulus, the Roman proconsul, who converted to Christianity after witnessing Paul's powerful preaching. From there, they sailed to Perga in Pamphylia, where Barnabas left Paul to continue alone, venturing into Pisidia, where he preached in synagogues, facing acceptance and rejection.

Second Missionary Journey (49-52 CE):

Paul's second journey, again accompanied by Barnabas, took him through various regions, including Cilicia, Galatia, Phrygia, and Mysia. He encountered significant opposition, particularly in Lystra, where he and Barnabas were mistaken for gods and stoned. However, Paul's resilience prevailed, and he continued his mission, leaving a lasting impact on the emerging Christian communities in these regions.

Third Missionary Journey (53-58 CE):

This extensive journey, the most significant in terms of its impact on the spread of Christianity, saw Paul establish churches in various parts of Asia Minor, including Ephesus, where he spent two years actively preaching and teaching, establishing a thriving Christian community. During his time in Ephesus, Paul faced opposition from silversmiths who feared the decline of their trade due to the growing influence of Christianity. However, Paul's powerful preaching and the spread of the Gospel continued unabated, solidifying Ephesus as a major center of early Christianity.

Journey to Rome (60-62 CE):

Paul's final journey, culminating in his arrival in Rome, was marked by two years of imprisonment in Caesarea Maritima. There, he faced accusations and challenges from Jewish leaders who sought to silence his influence. However, Paul's unwavering faith and eloquence prevailed, and he was ultimately allowed to travel to Rome, where he was initially placed under house arrest.

Paul's Imprisonment and Legacy:

While imprisoned in Rome, Paul continued to write letters, his words reaching far beyond the confines of his cell, nurturing and guiding Christian communities across the Roman Empire. His letters, preserved in the New Testament, stand as testaments to his unwavering faith, profound theological insights, and enduring legacy as a pivotal figure in the early church.

Paul's Death and the Enduring Impact of His Legacy:

The details surrounding Paul's death remain shrouded in mystery, but tradition holds that he was executed in Rome during the reign of Emperor Nero. His death, while tragic, did not diminish his influence; instead, it served to solidify his status as a martyr for the Christian faith.

Paul's life, journeys, and writings continue to inspire and challenge Christians today. His unwavering dedication to the Gospel message, courage in the face of adversity, and profound theological insights offer a timeless legacy that continues to shape the Christian faith. His commitment to the inclusion of the Gentiles, his powerful articulation of the concept of justification by faith, and his tireless efforts to establish churches across diverse regions have left an indelible mark on the history of Christianity, establishing him as one of the most influential figures in the early church.His unwavering faith, his courage in the face of adversity, and his profound theological insights continue to inspire believers today. They remind us of the transformative power of the

Gospel message and the enduring legacy of one man's dedication to sharing it with the world.

Paul's teachings, both orally and through his written epistles, were pivotal in shaping the evolving Christian faith and navigating complex theological and cultural terrain. While deeply rooted in the Jewish faith, his teachings expanded upon and adapted core concepts, addressing the emerging needs and challenges of the early Christian communities.

Justification by Faith:
Perhaps Paul's most enduring theological contribution was his articulation of the concept of justification by faith. Breaking with the traditional Jewish belief that salvation was achieved through adherence to the Mosaic Law, Paul asserted that faith in Jesus Christ, a gift of God's grace, was the sole means of receiving forgiveness and entering a right relationship with God.

The Law and Grace:
Paul's understanding of the Law as a guidepost rather than a path to salvation was revolutionary. He recognized the Law's role in revealing humanity's sinfulness and pointing to the need for a redeemer, but he also emphasized that the Law's limitations could only be overcome through the grace offered by Jesus Christ.

The Nature of Christ:
Paul's teachings on the nature of Christ were profound and influential, shaping the foundations of Christian theology. He viewed Jesus Christ as both fully God and fully human, the embodiment of the divine presence and the ultimate sacrifice for humanity's sins.

The Body of Christ:
Paul's concept of the Church as the "Body of Christ" was an innovative and powerful metaphor. He saw the Christian community as a unified organism,

with everyone playing a vital role in the collective mission of spreading the Gospel message. He emphasized the importance of love, unity, and mutual support among believers, recognizing the inherent value of everyone as a member of the Body of Christ.

The Importance of Spiritual Gifts:
Paul recognized that the Holy Spirit, a divine gift bestowed upon believers, enabled individuals to perform various spiritual services and ministries. He encouraged the development of spiritual gifts, such as prophecy, healing, and teaching, believing that these gifts were instrumental in building up the Christian community and spreading the Gospel message.

The Role of Women in the Church:
While acknowledging the cultural norms of his time, Paul's views on the role of women in the Church were complex and sometimes contested. He acknowledged the significant contributions of women in the early church, but he also urged them to avoid certain roles that were considered inappropriate for women in the broader society.

Paul's Influence on Early Christian Thought:
Paul's teachings, both oral and written, exerted a profound influence on the development of early Christian thought and practice. His bold articulation of justification by faith, his nuanced understanding of the Law and grace, and his insightful teachings on the nature of Christ, the Body of Christ, and spiritual gifts profoundly shaped the foundations of Christian theology.

Paul's Legacy and the Enduring Impact of His Teachings:
Despite the challenges and controversies surrounding his teachings, Paul's legacy remains strong as a visionary theologian and a pivotal figure in the early church. His bold interpretations of the Law, his powerful articulation of grace and justification by faith, and his emphasis on the unifying power of the Gospel message continue to inspire and challenge Christians today.

Paul's relationship with the early Christian community was complex and multifaceted, characterized by periods of collaboration, mutual support, and, at times, conflict. While he was a staunch defender of the Gospel message and a pivotal figure in its spread, his unique perspectives and innovative theological ideas sometimes clashed with the views of other early church leaders.

Collaboration and Mutual Support:
Despite differences in approach and perspectives, Paul collaborated with other early church leaders, notably Peter, James, and John, to promote spreading the Gospel message. They engaged in open dialogue and sought to resolve disagreements, recognizing the importance of unity within the emerging Christian community.

The Jerusalem Council:
One of the most significant instances of collaboration occurred in the Jerusalem Council, where Paul, accompanied by Barnabas, sought guidance on the issue of Gentile inclusion. Despite initial resistance from Jewish Christians who insisted on adherence to the Mosaic Law, the council ultimately reached a consensus, affirming that Gentiles could become Christians without undergoing circumcision or conforming to Jewish dietary laws.

Differences in Approach and Perspectives:
Paul's emphasis on grace rather than works and his inclusion of the Gentiles created tensions with some early Christian leaders who advocated for stricter adherence to Jewish law. This difference in approach led to disagreements and challenges, highlighting the complexities of transitioning from a predominantly Jewish faith to a global religion embracing diverse cultures and backgrounds.

The "Epistle to the Galatians":

One of Paul's most famous letters, His Epistle to the Galatians, eloquently and forcefully defends his theological perspective. In this letter, he passionately argues against those who sought to impose Jewish law on Gentile Christians, emphasizing that salvation is a gift of grace, not a reward for adherence to religious practices.

The Importance of Unity:

Paul recognized the importance of unity within the early Christian community. Despite theological differences and occasional disagreements, he maintained a spirit of cooperation, urging believers to embrace unity in the face of external threats and internal divisions.

Paul's Legacy and the Importance of Dialogue:

The complexities of Paul's relationship with the early church highlight the importance of open dialogue, mutual respect, and collaboration in navigating theological and cultural differences within the Christian faith. His willingness to engage in debate and his commitment to seeking unity serve as valuable lessons for contemporary Christians grappling with a wide range of theological and social issues.

Paul's enduring impact on the early church was immense. His missionary journeys, his profound theological insights, and his passionate defense of the Gospel message paved the way for the spread of Christianity beyond Jewish communities, shaping the foundations of a truly global religion. His legacy continues to inspire and challenge Christians today, reminding us of the transformative power of faith, the courage needed to confront adversity, and the importance of open dialogue and collaboration in fostering unity and understanding within the Christian community.

11.   THE SPREAD OF CHRISTIANITY TO DIVERSE REGIONS

The spread of Christianity beyond the confines of Jerusalem marked a pivotal chapter in the faith's evolution. This expansion was fueled by the tireless efforts of the Apostles, particularly Paul, who championed reaching out to the Gentiles. The journey from Jerusalem to Antioch, a vibrant city in modern-day Turkey, proved to be a turning point. Antioch served as a springboard for the Gospel's outreach, attracting a diverse population of Jews and Gentiles and becoming a hub for early Christian missions.

The apostle Paul, initially known as Saul, was a Jewish Pharisee who initially persecuted Christians. However, a profound encounter with the risen Christ transformed his life, turning him into a fervent apostle. Paul embarked on extensive missionary journeys, traveling across the Roman Empire and establishing churches in strategic cities like Ephesus, Corinth, and Rome. He encountered diverse cultures, languages, and belief systems, adapting his message to resonate with various audiences.

Paul's ministry wasn't without challenges. He faced opposition from Jewish leaders who saw his outreach to Gentiles as a threat to their traditions. He endured imprisonment, beatings, and even shipwrecks, but his unwavering faith and commitment to the Gospel remained steadfast. His writings, eloquently preserved in the New Testament, offer a window into the early church's struggles and triumphs.

Establishing churches in diverse regions, from Antioch to Ephesus to Rome, the early Christian communities marked a significant turning point. These communities were vibrant and diverse, attracting individuals from various social backgrounds and cultural influences. Early Christians, often facing persecution, found solace and fellowship in these communities. They formed a new social fabric, offering support to the poor and marginalized and challenging the rigid social hierarchies of the Roman Empire.

The spread of Christianity to Rome held special significance. Rome, as the heart of the Roman Empire, was a melting pot of cultures and ideologies. While Christianity initially faced persecution under Roman emperors, the message's strength and the early Christians' resilience contributed to its gradual acceptance. The city of Rome became a center of power and influence for the developing Christian church, drawing in individuals from diverse backgrounds and contributing to the church's growth.

The diverse cultural influences encountered by early Christians played a significant role in shaping the faith. While the core teachings remained constant, the practice of Christianity adapted to local customs and traditions. Early Christians incorporated elements of Roman and Greek culture into their worship practices, adopting forms of art, architecture, and literature. This fusion of cultures allowed Christianity to connect with diverse communities, further accelerating its spread.

In the years that followed, the spread of Christianity reached beyond the Roman Empire's borders. The Gospel message traveled to regions like Persia, Ethiopia, and India, encountering diverse cultural landscapes and interacting with other belief systems. The early Christians, driven by their commitment to the Gospel, found ways to adapt their message to resonate with different cultures, establishing new faith communities across vast geographical regions.

The geographic expansion of Christianity was not merely a physical phenomenon. It represented the transformative power of the Gospel to transcend cultural boundaries, drawing individuals from diverse backgrounds into a shared belief system. The journey from Jerusalem to Rome, from Antioch to Ephesus, and beyond, marked the beginning of a global faith, one that continues to evolve and adapt to the complexities of the modern world.

12. THE IMPACT OF EARLY CHRISTIAN COMMUNITIES ON SOCIETY

The early Christian communities, burgeoning in the midst of the Roman Empire, were not merely isolated groups of believers. They were active agents of change, weaving their faith into the social fabric of their world. Their impact extended beyond personal faith, leaving a lasting imprint on the realms of charity, education, and social reform.

Early Christian communities' unwavering commitment to charity was one of the most remarkable aspects. The Gospel message, emphasizing love, compassion, and service to the poor, found tangible expression in the daily lives of believers. In a society marked by significant disparities in wealth and social status, early Christians embraced a radical concept: equal worth of all human beings. This conviction fueled their tireless efforts to care for the marginalized and the needy, creating a vibrant network of charitable assistance that starkly contrasted the prevailing social order.

The early Christians established soup kitchens and shelters, providing food and refuge to the homeless, the sick, and the orphaned. They offered practical assistance to those in need, regardless of their social standing or religious background. This spirit of generosity, rooted in their belief in the radical inclusivity of God's love, transformed countless individuals' lives and challenged Roman society's prevailing norms.

Their commitment to education was another defining characteristic of early Christian communities. While the Roman Empire boasted impressive learning institutions, access to education was largely restricted to the elite. Early Christians believed that knowledge of God's word and understanding of Christian teachings were essential for all.

This belief fueled the establishment of schools and libraries within Christian communities, making education accessible to all who sought it. These schools went beyond mere literacy instruction, fostering a deep understanding of the Bible and Christian teachings. Through these educational initiatives, early Christians empowered individuals, providing them with the tools to engage with their faith and participate in the broader intellectual landscape of their time.

However, the path of the early Christians was not without its challenges. Their commitment to social justice and their refusal to conform to pagan rituals often led to persecution and hostility from the Roman authorities. The early Christians faced imprisonment, torture, and even martyrdom for their faith.

Despite the formidable obstacles, the early Christians persevered, and their faith strengthened by the shared struggles and triumphs they experienced. They drew inspiration from the example of Jesus, who had faced suffering and persecution for his message of love and justice.

Their commitment to love and compassion never wavered in the face of adversity. They extended their care to those who persecuted them, demonstrating the transformative power of their faith. This radical approach to love and forgiveness became a hallmark of early Christianity left a lasting legacy of compassion and forgiveness that would shape the course of history.

The impact of early Christian communities on the social fabric of the Roman Empire was profound and multifaceted. Through their commitment to charity, their pursuit of education, and their relentless advocacy for social justice, they challenged the established order and offered a vision of a world transformed by love, compassion, and equality. Their unwavering dedication to their faith and their unwavering commitment to serve others in a world often characterized by indifference and cruelty left an enduring legacy that continues to inspire and challenge us today.

13. CHALLENGES AND PERSECUTIONS FACED BY EARLY CHRISTIANS

The early Christians, united by their faith in Jesus Christ, faced a formidable array of challenges, both from the outside world and from within their own ranks. With its vast power and complex social structures, the Roman Empire presented a formidable obstacle to the nascent Christian community. Roman authorities viewed Christianity as a subversive force, a threat to the established order, and the imperial cult that served as the foundation of Roman society.

Early Christians were often accused of atheism, as they refused to acknowledge the Roman gods and the emperor as divine figures. They were also accused of practicing cannibalism due to their partaking in the Eucharist, a ritual that symbolized the body and blood of Christ. The Roman government, determined to maintain control and unity within the empire, persecuted Christians, subjecting them to imprisonment, torture, and even execution.

The brutal reality of Roman persecution is vividly illustrated in the writings of early Christians. The accounts of martyrs who died for their faith are filled with graphic descriptions of suffering and resilience. One chilling example is the martyrdom of Saint Stephen, who was stoned to death for his unwavering belief in Jesus Christ. Another harrowing account details the persecution of Christians under the Roman Emperor Nero, who blamed them for a devastating fire in Rome and ordered their public executions in the most brutal manner imaginable. These stories, while grim, serve as powerful reminders of the unwavering faith and courage exhibited by early Christians in the face of relentless persecution.

Beyond the Roman authorities, early Christians also faced significant opposition from within their own societies. Jewish communities, from whom the Christian faith initially emerged, often viewed Christianity as a heretical offshoot of Judaism. This animosity stemmed from the Christian rejection of certain Jewish laws and traditions, particularly the belief that Jesus was the Messiah. The early Christians, however, understood that Jesus fulfilled the prophecies of the Jewish scriptures and was the long-awaited savior. This fundamental difference in interpretation led to friction and, in some cases, open conflict between Jews and early Christians.

The early Christians, however, were not solely defined by their opposition to the Roman Empire and their sometimes-tense relationships with Jewish communities. They were also a community in constant flux, grappling with internal disputes and differences in understanding. The emergence of Christianity as a new religious movement led to theological debates about the nature of Jesus Christ, the role of the Holy Spirit, and the interpretation of scripture. These debates, often passionate and intense, reflected the complexities of the early Christian faith, which was rapidly evolving as it spread to new regions and cultures.

The most significant internal debate centered on the question of whether the Gospel message was intended for Jews only or if it should be extended to Gentiles (non-Jews). This issue, known as the "Judaizer Controversy", pitted those who believed in the necessity of Jewish law for salvation against those who advocated for a more inclusive approach. The Apostle Paul, a key figure in expanding Christianity beyond Jewish communities, became a central figure in this debate. Paul, originally a persecutor of Christians, experienced a life-changing conversion and thereafter dedicated his life to spreading the Gospel message. Paul, through his journeys and writings, argued that salvation was available to all through faith in Jesus Christ, regardless of their ethnicity or background.

Paul's efforts to bridge the divide between Jewish and Gentile believers played a crucial role in the growth and expansion of Christianity. However, this approach also caused significant controversy. Many Jewish Christians clung to the traditional Jewish practices and felt that Paul's teachings were too radical. This debate was ultimately resolved through the Council of Jerusalem, an early gathering of Christian leaders, where it was decided that Gentile Christians were not obligated to adhere to Jewish law. However, the Council also insisted that Gentiles should abstain from certain practices considered pagan, such as idolatry and eating blood. This compromise paved the way for the growth of the Christian church within Gentile communities.

The early Christians faced not only external persecution and internal theological debates but also the challenges of establishing a cohesive community in a world that often looked upon them with suspicion and hostility. As Christianity spread, it encountered diverse cultures, each with its own set of values and traditions. This created a complex landscape for the early Christians as they sought to maintain their faith while engaging with the broader world.

In the early centuries, Christian communities developed distinct forms of organization, leadership, and worship practices. While initially structured around the model of the Jewish synagogue, the Christian church evolved to suit the needs of its growing membership. The emergence of bishops, presbyters (elders), and deacons, who held leadership positions within the church, reflected the need for a structured organization to guide and shepherd the expanding community. The development of these roles, alongside establishing church councils, contributed to the growth of church authority and governance, laying the foundation for the future structure of the Christian church.

As Christianity spread, the early Christians also faced the challenge of developing a distinctive identity amidst the diverse religious landscape of the Roman world. They had to define their beliefs, practices, and values in relation to the dominant Roman paganism and other emerging religions. The early Christians, deeply devoted to their faith, often clashed with the existing Roman social and religious norms. This clash, however, also led to the development of distinct Christian practices and traditions that would shape the future of the faith.

The early Christians engaged in various forms of charitable work, providing assistance to the sick, poor, and marginalized within their communities. They established hospices, hospitals, and soup kitchens, demonstrating their compassion and commitment to serving the needs of those in distress. This emphasis on compassion and service, rooted in the teachings of Jesus, became a cornerstone of the Christian worldview.

The early Christians also developed a rich artistic and literary tradition that expressed their faith and values. They created hymns, poems, and writings that reflected their understanding of the Christian message and their faith experiences. These writings, which included letters, sermons, and theological treatises, played a crucial role in shaping Christian thought and practice. These early writings, often written in Greek and Latin, contributed to the emergence of a distinct Christian literature that would influence future generations of believers.

The early Christians faced significant challenges in the Roman Empire, but their resilience and dedication to their faith ultimately led to the growth and spread of Christianity. The Christian message, emphasizing love, compassion, forgiveness, and hope, resonated with many people, leading to the conversion of individuals from all walks of life.

Despite their hardships, the early Christians demonstrated extraordinary courage and determination. They refused to compromise their faith, even when faced with threats of imprisonment, torture, and death. Their unwavering belief in Jesus Christ and their commitment to spreading the Gospel message transformed the world.

The early Christians, through their perseverance and unwavering commitment laid the foundations for the future of the Christian church. They established communities, developed theological doctrines, and created practices that would shape the course of Christianity for centuries to come. The challenges they encountered, both from external sources and within their own ranks, only strengthened their resolve and refined their faith. Their story, a testament to the transformative power of belief, continues to inspire and guide believers today.

14.   THE EMERGENCE OF EARLY CHRISTIAN THEOLOGY

The nascent Christian community, fueled by the transformative message of Jesus' life, death, and resurrection, was grappling with profound questions about the nature of God, the significance of Jesus' identity, and the meaning of salvation. This period witnessed the emergence of early Christian theology, a vibrant and often contested process of grappling with these essential questions.

The foundations of early Christian theology were laid by the Apostles and their disciples, who sought to understand and articulate the implications of Jesus' teachings and the profound experience of his resurrection. The early Christians were deeply rooted in their Jewish heritage, drawing heavily on the Old Testament scriptures to interpret Jesus' life and mission. They saw him as the fulfillment of Jewish prophecy, the promised Messiah who had come to redeem humanity from sin.

The Trinity: A Triune God

One of the earliest and most pivotal theological concepts to emerge was the doctrine of the Trinity. Early Christians, reflecting on Jesus' teachings and the experience of the Holy Spirit, came to understand God as a triune being: Father, Son, and Holy Spirit. The Trinity, however, wasn't a neatly defined concept from the outset. Initial attempts to articulate it often drew criticism and led to heated debates within the nascent church.

The concept of a single God existing in three distinct persons—Father, Son, and Holy Spirit—was a radical departure from traditional Jewish monotheism. Early Christians grappled with how to reconcile God's unity with Jesus's and the Holy Spirit's distinct personhood. The emergence of the Trinity doctrine was a gradual process, shaped by scriptural interpretation, theological reflection, and the need to address emerging heresies.

Christology: The Nature of Christ

Closely intertwined with the doctrine of the Trinity was the question of Christology—the understanding of Jesus' identity. Early Christians acknowledged Jesus' divine nature, proclaiming him as the Son of God. However, they also struggled with the question of Jesus' human nature. Was he fully divine, fully human, or a combination of both?

The debate over Christ's identity was particularly intense in the early centuries. Some argued that Jesus was merely a human being God chose for a special mission. Others asserted his divinity, seeing him as God in human form. This ongoing discussion led to the development of different Christological doctrines, shaping the understanding of Jesus' nature and his role in salvation.

The Atonement: Reconciliation with God

Another crucial theological concept that emerged in the early church was the doctrine of atonement, which focused on how humanity could be reconciled with God. Early Christians recognized that humanity's sinfulness had created a chasm between them and God, a barrier that needed to be bridged. They looked to Jesus' sacrifice on the cross as the means of atonement, seeing his death as a propitiatory offering to God that reconciled humanity to him.

The concept of atonement was multifaceted, with various interpretations emerging in the early church. Some emphasized the idea of Jesus' death as a ransom paid to the devil to liberate humanity from his power. Others saw it as a sacrificial act that satisfied God's justice and paved the way for reconciliation. The development of atonement theology was deeply intertwined with the understanding of sin, human nature, and the nature of God's justice.

15. THEOLOGICAL DEBATES AND THE EMERGENCE OF ORTHODOXY

The early church was a cauldron of theological debate, with various perspectives emerging on key doctrines like the Trinity, Christology, and atonement. These debates were often fueled by theological differences, cultural influences, and the need to address emerging heresies. Heresy, in the early church, referred to beliefs that deviated significantly from the accepted teachings of the Christian community.

Theologians like Justin Martyr, Clement of Alexandria, and Origen attempted to articulate Christian faith in a way that was consistent with the scriptures and addressed the challenges posed by philosophical and cultural influences. These early theologians often engaged in reasoned dialogue and wrote extensively to defend their perspectives and address challenges to orthodox belief.

The need to address theological controversies and define Christian doctrine led to the convening of early church councils, such as the Council of Jerusalem and the Council of Nicaea. These councils, composed of prominent bishops and theologians, sought to reach a consensus on contested issues and establish a unified understanding of the Christian faith.

The Council of Nicaea and the Definition of the Trinity

One of the most significant events in the development of early Christian theology was the Council of Nicaea in 325 AD. Convened by Emperor Constantine, the council was tasked with addressing the Arian controversy, which challenged the divinity of Christ. After intense debates, the council condemned Arianism and affirmed Christ's full divinity, declaring him to be "God from God, Light from Light, true God from true God."

The Council of Nicaea's decision had a profound impact on the development of Christian theology. It established a foundational principle of Christian belief—the full divinity of Christ—and solidified the doctrine of the Trinity. The Nicene Creed, drafted by the council, became a cornerstone of the Christian faith, adopted by various Christian denominations, and served as a defining statement of their beliefs.

The Ongoing Evolution of Christian Theology

The development of early Christian theology was shaped by the need to interpret scripture, address theological controversies, and respond to cultural influences. The early church fathers' writings and teachings provided a foundation for subsequent theological developments. Their insights into the nature of God, the person of Christ, and the means of salvation continue to be studied and debated by theologians today.

The emergence of early Christian theology was a complex and often contentious process that was essential to establishing a coherent Christian faith. Through the articulation of key doctrines, engagement in theological debates, and the convening of church councils, early Christians laid the groundwork for the vast tapestry of Christian thought that continues to evolve and unfold today.

16. THE ROLE OF SCRIPTURE IN EARLY
CHRISTIANITY

The early Christians, seeking to understand their newfound faith, looked to the Hebrew Scriptures, the foundation of their Jewish heritage, for guidance and meaning. This sacred text, known as the Old Testament to Christians, became a vital source of inspiration and interpretation for their understanding of Jesus, his message, and the nature of God. They saw in the Old Testament prophecies fulfilled in the life and ministry of Jesus, confirming his identity as the Messiah and the Son of God. The stories of the prophets, particularly their calls for justice, compassion, and God's love for the downtrodden, resonated deeply with early Christians. The Psalms, with their praise, lament, and hope expressions, provided a rich source of devotional reflection and theological insight.

However, alongside the Old Testament, a new body of writings began to emerge – the writings that would later be recognized as the New Testament. These writings, largely penned by the Apostles and their companions, chronicled the life and teachings of Jesus, the spread of the Gospel, and the early church's experiences and challenges. This collection of texts, known as the New Testament, became a vital source of authority for early Christians, alongside the Old Testament.

However, the process of selecting and canonizing these writings was not simple or straightforward. As Christianity spread, various Christian communities emerged with their own collections of writings that they considered authoritative. Some writings were accepted more widely than others, while some were disputed or rejected altogether. Several factors influenced the selection process.

17. APOSTOLIC AUTHORITY:

Writings attributed to the Apostles, especially those who had personally known Jesus, held significant weight. The Gospels, attributed to Matthew, Mark, Luke, and John, each offering a unique perspective on Jesus' life and ministry, were widely accepted as authoritative.

Conformity to Orthodox Teachings:
As the early church grappled with theological controversies, writings that affirmed the central tenets of faith – the divinity of Christ, the Trinity, and the resurrection – gained wider acceptance. The epistles of Paul, addressing various issues like salvation, church life, and ethics, were particularly influential in shaping Christian thought and practice.

Liturgical Usage:
Writings that were regularly used in worship and church gatherings gained prominence and authority. The Book of Acts, detailing the spread of the Gospel and the early church's experiences, became a central text for understanding Christian history and mission.

Testimony and Tradition:
Writings that had been used and passed down through generations of Christians, particularly those that prominent church leaders and councils affirmed, were given greater weight.

The selection process gradually involved various local churches, councils, and individual leaders. The first official canonization of the New Testament, recognizing a specific set of 27 books as authoritative, occurred in the late fourth century. This event marked a significant milestone in the development of Christianity, providing a unified and definitive collection of sacred writings for all Christians to follow.

The emergence of the New Testament canon was not without its controversies. Some writings were initially accepted in some churches but later excluded. The debate regarding the inclusion or exclusion of writings, such as the Book of Revelation, continued for centuries. However, the eventual canonization of the New Testament marked a crucial step in the development of Christian theology and practice.

It provided a foundation for doctrinal development, offering a unified narrative about Jesus, his teachings, and the nature of faith. The New Testament became the basis for Christian worship, providing hymns, prayers, and liturgical texts that guided the church's worship life. It served as a source of moral guidance, shaping Christian ethics and providing principles for living a life aligned with God's will.

The New Testament also became a vital tool for evangelism and mission, providing a clear message about Jesus and the promise of salvation to be shared with others. The letters of Paul, addressing various issues of faith and practice, became essential guides for establishing and nurturing Christian communities.

The impact of the Old and New Testaments on the early church was profound and lasting. The Jewish Scriptures provided a rich historical and theological context for understanding Jesus and his message, while the writings of the Apostles and their companions offered a firsthand account of Jesus' life, teachings, and the beginnings of the Christian movement. Together, these writings provided a foundation for Christian theology, practice, and mission, shaping the development of the church and its enduring impact on history.

18. THE IMPACT OF GREEK PHILOSOPHY ON EARLY CHRISTIAN BELIEFS

The fusion of Christian beliefs with the intellectual currents of the Hellenistic world was a defining moment in the development of early Christianity. While the core message of Jesus remained central, the encounter with Greek philosophy profoundly influenced how early Christians understood their faith and articulated it to a broader audience. This intellectual engagement shaped the development of Christian theology, offering a framework for understanding the divine, the nature of Christ, and the meaning of salvation.

One of the key figures in this intellectual synthesis was Justin Martyr(c. 100-165 AD). As a former Stoic philosopher, Justin brought a philosophical mindset to his embrace of Christianity. He saw Jesus's teachings as fulfilling the Old Testament's promises and providing a rational and ethical framework for living. In his writings, notably Dialogue with Trypho, Justin argued that Christian beliefs could be harmonized with Greek philosophical thought, demonstrating the Christian faith's rationality to Jews and pagans. He embraced the notion of logos, the divine reason or word, as a bridge between the divine and the human, arguing that the Logos was embodied in the person of Jesus Christ. This idea, rooted in Stoic philosophy, provided a foundation for Christian understanding of the relationship between God and the world.

Another significant figure was Clement of Alexandria (c.150-215 AD), a prominent Christian scholar and teacher. Clement sought to reconcile Christianity with the intellectual heritage of classical Greek culture. He believed that the Gospel message was not only for the common people but also for educated individuals and that Greek wisdom, properly understood, could lead to a deeper appreciation of Christian truth. He argued that Christian faith and Greek philosophy were not incompatible but complementary, as they shared a common quest for wisdom and truth. Clement's emphasis on the importance of education and the use of reason in understanding Christianity paved the way for developing Christian theology as a systematic discipline.

Origen (c. 185-254 AD), a brilliant and influential theologian, further integrated Greek philosophy into Christian thought. He was heavily influenced by Platonism, particularly its concept of the eternal and unchanging nature of the divine. Origen developed a complex theology of the Trinity, drawing on Platonic ideas about the unity and diversity of the divine nature. He also applied philosophical principles to the interpretation of Scripture, arguing that the Bible contained multiple levels of meaning, accessible to different levels of understanding. While controversial in its time, Origen's work had a lasting influence on Christian theology, paving the way for the development of allegorical interpretation and integrating philosophical concepts into theological discussions.

The impact of Greek philosophy on early Christian thought was multifaceted. It provided a framework for understanding the relationship between God and the world, the nature of Christ, and the meaning of salvation. It also fostered the development of Christian theology as a reasoned and systematic discipline. While some early Christians, like Tertullian, rejected the influence of pagan philosophy, arguing for the supremacy of Scripture, the intellectual engagement with Greek thought ultimately led to the emergence of a more sophisticated and comprehensive Christian worldview.

The influence of Greek philosophy was not without its challenges. As Christianity spread beyond its Jewish roots, the need to articulate its message in the language of the Roman world became increasingly important. This led to debates about the compatibility of Christian faith with Greek philosophical ideas, resulting in various interpretations and understandings. The struggle to reconcile Christian theology with Greek philosophy shaped the development of Christian thought and gave rise to diverse schools of interpretation.

The encounter between Christianity and Greek philosophy, however, was not a one-way street. The influence went both ways, as Christian thought also shaped and informed the development of later philosophical ideas. For instance, the Christian concept of love deeply influenced the development of Christian ethics and significantly impacted Western philosophical thought.

The influence of Greek philosophy on early Christian thought remains a significant topic of study for historians and theologians. Understanding this intellectual encounter helps us grasp the complexities of early Christianity, the development of Christian theology, and how the faith was shaped by its engagement with the broader cultural landscape of the ancient world.

19. THE FORMATION OF CHRISTIAN RITUALS AND PRACTICES

The development of early Christian rituals and practices was a fascinating tapestry woven from threads of Jewish tradition, Roman influence, and the evolving understanding of the Gospel message. As the Christian community expanded beyond its initial Jewish roots, it encountered a diverse range of cultural and religious practices, which inevitably influenced the formation of its own distinctive rituals.

One of the most significant early Christian rituals was baptism. This practice, rooted in Jewish ritual purification, took on new meaning within the Christian context. It symbolized the cleansing of sins and the symbolic death and resurrection of the believer with Christ. Early Christians saw baptism as a crucial step in entering the Christian community, a public declaration of faith, and a commitment to a new life in Christ. The practice of baptism, often performed in rivers or pools, reflected the belief in the cleansing power of water, drawing parallels with the cleansing of the Israelites at the Red Sea and the baptism of Jesus by John the Baptist.

Another foundational ritual was communion, also known as the Lord's Supper or Eucharist. This practice evolved from the Jewish tradition of the Passover meal, where bread and wine were shared in remembrance of the Exodus. For early Christians, however, communion held a profound significance, symbolizing the body and blood of Christ, offered for the atonement of sins. The shared meal became a sacred act, a reminder of Christ's sacrifice, and a communal expression of faith and unity. The early Christian practice of communal meals, often accompanied by prayers and hymns, reflected the importance of fellowship and sharing in the Christian community.

Prayer was central in early Christian life, both private and communal. Inspired by Jewish prayer traditions, Christians regularly prayed to God, seeking guidance, forgiveness, and intercession. The practice of prayer involved personal reflection, communal worship, and the invocation of Jesus' name. Early Christians frequently met for prayer, often in homes or in small gatherings, building a sense of community and spiritual unity. Their prayers often focused on themes of repentance, praise, and petitions for God's blessings.

Worship, the collective expression of faith, emerged as a distinct practice within the early Christian community. While initially resembling Jewish synagogue services, with readings from the Hebrew Scriptures and prayers, Christian worship gradually developed its own distinctive elements. Early Christians gathered on the first day of the week, the day of Christ's resurrection, to share meals, read Scripture, pray, and sing hymns. These gatherings, held in homes, catacombs, or other gathering places, provided a space for fellowship, spiritual nourishment, and the proclamation of the Gospel message.

The development of early Christian rituals and practices was not a static process. It was shaped by ongoing theological debates, cultural influences, and the evolving understanding of the Christian faith. Early church leaders, like Clement of Alexandria, Origen, and Augustine, played a pivotal role in shaping and refining these practices, drawing from Jewish and Roman traditions while incorporating the unique insights of the Christian faith.

As Christianity spread beyond its Jewish origins, it encountered a range of cultural and religious influences.Roman practices, such as the use of incense and the presence of images in worship, gradually seeped into Christian rituals.

The influence of Roman civic life, emphasizing order, hierarchy, and public gatherings, also contributed to the evolving structures of early Christian worship. Yet, despite these influences, early Christians remained committed to preserving the core elements of their faith, adapting their practices to new contexts while upholding the fundamental principles of their beliefs.

The formation of Christian rituals and practices was an organic process shaped by the shared experiences, theological insights, and evolving understanding of the early Christians. Their embrace of Jewish tradition and Roman influence while maintaining a distinctively Christian identity reflects the dynamic interplay of faith, culture, and history in forming one of the world's major religions. The rituals and practices that emerged in early church provided a framework for communal worship, spiritual nourishment, and the transmission of the Christian message. These practices, passed down through generations, continue to shape and inform Christian life and worship in the 21st century.

20. THE RISE OF EARLY CHURCH LEADERS AND THEIR INFLUENCE

The early Christian church witnessed the rise of influential figures who shaped its developing doctrines, practices, and organizational structure. These leaders emerged from diverse backgrounds and carried with them a wealth of experiences and insights, contributing to the vibrant tapestry of early Christianity.

Ignatius of Antioch, a prominent figure of the first century, was a disciple of the apostles and served as the bishop of Antioch. His writings offer a glimpse into the early church's struggles with Gnosticism, a philosophical movement that challenged traditional Christian beliefs. Ignatius fiercely defended the orthodox understanding of Christ's divinity, asserting that Christ was both fully divine and fully human. His letters, penned during his journey to Rome to face martyrdom, provide valuable insights into the early church's understanding of the Eucharist and the role of bishops in the church's governance.

Polycarp, another significant leader of the second century, was a disciple of the apostle John and bishop of Smyrna. He was known for his unwavering adherence to the apostles' teachings, which he meticulously preserved and passed on to his successors. His writings, though limited, provide a valuable window into the early church's practice of worship, its emphasis on moral conduct, and its understanding of Christ's teachings. Polycarp's martyrdom in 155 CE is a testament to the early church's willingness to suffer for their faith in the face of Roman persecution.

Irenaeus of Lyons, a key figure in developing Christian theology, was a bishop who tirelessly combated Gnostic heresies. His magnum opus, "Against Heresies," is a monumental work of early Christian literature, systematically refuting Gnostic doctrines and defending the orthodox Christian understanding of God, Christ, and the church. Irenaeus emphasized the importance of tradition and the church's role in preserving the apostles' teachings. His work laid the foundation for a systematic and comprehensive approach to Christian theology, demonstrating the intellectual rigor with which early Christians engaged with theological challenges.

Though diverse in their backgrounds and approaches, these early church leaders shared a common commitment to spreading the Gospel message and safeguarding the integrity of the Christian faith. Their writings and actions left an indelible mark on the early church, shaping its theological understanding, organizational structure, and response to its challenges.

Ignatius of Antioch's journey from a simple disciple to a prominent leader reflects the dynamic nature of the early church. His letters, penned while facing death, resonate with a powerful message of faith and unwavering commitment to the Christian faith. He was particularly concerned with the growing threat of Gnosticism, a philosophical movement that challenged traditional Christian beliefs about the nature of God and Christ. Ignatius saw Gnosticism as a dangerous deviation from the true Gospel message and vehemently defended the orthodox understanding of Christ's divinity. His letters, filled with passionate pleas for unity and fidelity to the apostles' teachings, became a powerful testament to the early church's struggle to maintain its identity amidst a diverse landscape of theological thought.

Polycarp's life and teachings embody the values of tradition and the importance of preserving the apostles' legacy. His connection to the apostle John, one of Jesus' closest disciples, highlights the strong connection between the early generations of Christians and the original followers of

Christ. Polycarp's unwavering adherence to the apostles' teachings was a bulwark against the emerging heresies that threatened the core tenets of Christian belief. His martyrdom, which he faced with courage and dignity, exemplified the early church's willingness to suffer for their faith in the face of Roman persecution. His life story serves as a poignant reminder of the enduring strength of faith in the face of adversity.

Irenaeus of Lyons, a skilled theologian and a tireless defender of orthodoxy, played a critical role in combating Gnostic heresies that threatened to undermine the foundations of Christianity. His masterpiece, "Against Heresies," is a meticulously crafted theological argument that systematically dismantles the Gnostic claims and defends the traditional Christian understanding of God, Christ, and the church. Irenaeus's work is a testament to the early church's intellectual rigor and commitment to defending its beliefs' integrity against the onslaught of diverse theological challenges. He emphasized the importance of tradition, arguing that the church's teachings were rooted in the apostolic succession, ensuring the continuity and authenticity of the Christian faith. His work laid the groundwork for a systematic and comprehensive approach to Christian theology, paving the way for future generations of theologians to engage in the ongoing exploration of the Christian faith.

These early church leaders, each with their unique contributions and challenges, collectively played a vital role in shaping the landscape of early Christianity. Their lives and teachings offer a window into the early church's struggles with theological diversity, its commitment to preserving the apostles' teachings, and its unwavering faith in the face of persecution. Their influence resonates within the Christian church today, inspiring believers to uphold the values of faith, unity, and enduring commitment to the Gospel message.

As the early Christian church grew and spread, it faced numerous challenges, ranging from internal disputes over theological doctrines to external pressures from the Roman Empire. These challenges forced early Christians to grapple with fundamental questions about their faith, relationship with the world, and role within Roman society. These struggles led to the development of theological doctrines, the establishment of church structures, and the formation of a distinct Christian identity that would shape the future of the faith.

The emergence of early church leaders like Ignatius, Polycarp, and Irenaeus was not just a response to these challenges but also a testament to the vitality and dynamism of the early Christian movement. These individuals, drawn from various backgrounds and with unique perspectives, brought their experiences, insights, and intellectual prowess to bear on the day's pressing issues. Their writings and actions became guiding lights for future generations of Christians, shaping the course of theological discourse and the emerging church's organizational structure.

Ignatius of Antioch, a fervent advocate for the church's unity, faced a double challenge: combating Gnostic heresies and navigating the growing tensions between the church and the Roman Empire. His letters, penned during his journey to Rome to face martyrdom, express a deep concern for preserving the true Gospel message and the unity of the Christian community. His writings offer valuable insights into the early church's understanding of the Eucharist and the role of bishops in governing the church, reflecting the developing structure and practices of the nascent Christian community.

Polycarp, a figure of great integrity and devotion, played a key role in preserving the apostles' teachings, ensuring the continuity of faith and tradition within the emerging church. His connection to the apostle John, a close disciple of Jesus, solidified his role as a bridge between the earliest generation of Christians and the subsequent generations who were grappling with the complexities of the developing Christian faith. His martyrdom, faced with courage and dignity, became a powerful symbol of early Christians' unwavering faith and resilience in the face of persecution. Polycarp's example, combined with his deep commitment to tradition, influenced the development of church leadership and the values of adherence to apostolic teachings that shaped the early church.

Irenaeus of Lyons, a towering figure in early Christian theology, emerged as a forceful defender of orthodoxy and a systematic thinker who sought to clarify and articulate the core tenets of Christian belief. His monumental work, "Against Heresies," is a comprehensive treatise refuting the Gnostic heresies that threatened the very foundations of Christian belief. Irenaeus's work is a testament to the early church's engagement with philosophical and theological challenges, demonstrating the intellectual rigor with which early Christians sought to understand and defend their faith. His emphasis on tradition and the church's role in preserving the apostles' teachings further solidified the importance of established leadership and the transmission of faith across generations.

The emergence of these influential leaders played a critical role in shaping the early Christian church. Their contributions to theological understanding, their leadership in combating heresies, and their unwavering commitment to the Gospel message became defining elements of the early church's journey. Their legacies continue to resonate within the Christian church today, reminding believers of the importance of upholding the core tenets of faith, embracing tradition, and engaging in the ongoing dialogue and exploration of theological concepts. Their examples serve as beacons of inspiration, guiding Christians through the complexities of faith, tradition, and the pursuit of a deeper understanding of the Gospel message.

21. THE ESTABLISHMENT OF THE CHURCH IN ROME

The seeds of Christianity in Rome were sown in a strategic location-a bustling metropolis, a melting pot of cultures and beliefs. The city's vast population, comprising diverse ethnicities and social classes, provided fertile ground for the Gospel's message of hope and salvation. It is believed that the first Christians in Rome were likely Jewish converts who had been influenced by the teachings of Jesus and his early followers. As the message of Christianity spread, it began to attract individuals from all walks of life, including members of the Roman aristocracy, slaves, and ordinary citizens.

One of the key factors that contributed to the rapid growth of Christianity in Rome was the city's extensive network of roads and trade routes. This network facilitated the movement of people and ideas, spreading the Gospel quickly throughout the empire. As Christians traveled for work, trade, or pilgrimage, they carried the message of their faith to new regions. The early Roman Christians formed vibrant communities where they shared their faith, supported one another, and practiced their beliefs. These communities often met in secret, as Christianity was initially viewed as a foreign religion and faced persecution.

Another crucial factor in the growth of Christianity in Rome was the presence of prominent Christian leaders, particularly Peter and Paul. Peter, considered the first Pope by the Roman Catholic Church, is believed to have traveled to Rome in the mid-first century. He established a strong presence in the city, becoming a leading figure in the early Christian community. Paul, who had previously been a persecutor of Christians, experienced a dramatic conversion and became a fervent apostle, spreading the Gospel message throughout the Mediterranean region. He is believed to have arrived in Rome in the 60s CE, where he was imprisoned and eventually executed.

The stories of Peter and Paul are deeply entwined with the history of the early church in Rome. Peter's ministry in the city is often associated with establishing the Roman Catholic Church, while Paul's missionary work and writings contributed significantly to the development of Christian theology and doctrine. Their presence in Rome lent a sense of authority and legitimacy to the burgeoning Christian community.

However, Christianity's growth in Rome was not without its challenges. The early Christians faced persecution from Roman authorities, who viewed their faith as a threat to the established order. The emperors Nero, Domitian, and others unleashed waves of persecution, which resulted in the imprisonment, torture, and execution of countless Christians. Despite these challenges, the Christian community in Rome persevered, finding strength and inspiration in their faith.

The resilience of the early Roman Christians was remarkable. They met secretly, shared their resources, and encouraged one another through periods of intense persecution. They faced their trials with courage and faith, knowing that their commitment to Jesus Christ would ultimately lead to a reward in the afterlife. Their unwavering belief in the Gospel message fueled the continued growth of Christianity in Rome despite the relentless opposition they faced.

The early Christian communities in Rome were not monolithic. They comprised diverse individuals with various backgrounds, beliefs, and practices. While enriching the faith, this diversity also led to internal tensions and debates. Theological disputes and disagreements about church organization and leadership emerged, reflecting the ongoing development of Christian thought and practice.

Despite these challenges, the early Christians in Rome laid the foundation for a vibrant and influential Christian community that would eventually become the center of Western Christendom. The city's strategic location, the ministries of prominent figures like Peter and Paul, and the resilience of the early Christians in the face of persecution all contributed to establishing a powerful and enduring Christian presence in Rome. This foundation would serve as a springboard for the further spread of Christianity throughout the Roman Empire and beyond, leaving an indelible mark on Western civilization and shaping the religious landscape of the world.

22. THE ROLE OF PETER AND PAUL IN ROME

The arrival of Peter and Paul in Rome marked a pivotal moment in the city's nascent Christian history. These two figures, central to the early church, brought with them a wealth of experience, authority, and the fervor of the early Christian movement. Their ministries in Rome, though brief, left an indelible mark on the development of the Roman church and its trajectory within the larger Christian community.

Peter, known as the "rock" upon which Jesus built his Church, was one of the twelve apostles and had a profound impact on early Christianity. He was the first to preach the gospel to the Jewish people and witnessed Jesus' miracles and resurrection firsthand. Peter's authority among the early Christians was undeniable, and he is credited with leading the first Christian community in Jerusalem.

While the precise details surrounding Peter's arrival in Rome remain shrouded in historical uncertainty, tradition holds that he came to the city in the mid-40s CE, possibly seeking refuge from persecution in Jerusalem. According to Eusebius, a fourth-century historian, Peter arrived in Rome during the reign of Claudius, who had expelled Jews from the city. This expulsion likely included Jewish Christians like Peter, forcing him to seek a new home and continue his ministry.

Upon his arrival, Peter's ministry in Rome blossomed. He established a church, likely located on the Aventine Hill, which quickly attracted followers and spread Christ's message among Jews and Gentiles. While his ministry in Rome is shrouded in mystery, his presence was felt throughout the city. He

71

interacted with both Jewish and Gentile communities, attracting many to the Christian faith.

The presence of Peter in Rome is also intricately linked to the city's first Christian leadership. He served as a spiritual guide and mentor, shaping the faith of the nascent Roman church and its early leaders. Peter's influence extended beyond Rome, as his letters, particularly the first epistle, addressed concerns and offered guidance to Christians facing persecution across the Roman world.

Peter's ministry, however, was tragically cut short. He was martyred in Rome under the reign of Nero, likely during the great fire of 64 CE. This event solidified his status as a martyr and further cemented his importance in the hearts of Christians. His martyrdom, along with the persecution of Christians, became a powerful symbol of their unwavering faith and their willingness to die for their beliefs.

Unlike Peter, Paul was not one of the original twelve apostles. He was a Jewish scholar who was initially a fervent opponent of Christianity but underwent a dramatic conversion experience on the road to Damascus. After his conversion, Paul became a missionary, spreading the Gospel message to diverse regions, particularly among Gentiles. His journeys and epistles form the foundation of the New Testament and significantly shaped early Christian theology and practice.

According to historical accounts, Paul arrived in Rome around 60 CE. He was brought to the city as a prisoner, accused of inciting sedition and awaiting trial before Caesar Nero. During his imprisonment, Paul did not remain silent.His imprisonment allowed him to continue his ministry, preaching the Gospel to both Jews and Gentiles in Rome. He received visitors from various Christian communities, sharing his insights and guidance, and even wrote several of his epistles, including Ephesians, Philippians, and Colossians, while under house arrest.

Paul's ministry in Rome profoundly impacted the city's Christian community. He attracted a large following, including both Jews and Gentiles, and established a church within the city. His teachings, emphasizing the grace of God and the universal availability of salvation, resonated deeply with the Roman populace. He also engaged in theological debates, engaged with Jewish leaders, and promoted the inclusion of Gentiles within the Christian community.

While Paul's trial remains shrouded in historical uncertainty, tradition suggests he faced the same fate as Peter: martyrdom under Nero. He was likely executed in 67 CE, adding to the growing number of Christian martyrs in the city. His death, like Peter's, served as a testament to his unwavering faith and the growing persecution faced by Christians in Rome.

The ministries of Peter and Paul in Rome are often seen as foundational to the city's Christian community. Their lives and teachings contributed significantly to the growth and development of the Roman church, shaping its theological outlook and organizational structure. Their martyrdom served as a powerful symbol of Christian faith and resilience, inspiring countless generations of Christians who faced persecution for their beliefs.

The influence of Peter and Paul extended beyond Rome's borders. Their writings and teachings shaped the development of Christian theology and practice throughout the Roman world. They played a significant role in establishing the organized Christian church's foundation and expansion beyond its initial Jewish context.

Peter and Paul's contributions to the early church in Rome were multifaceted. They strengthened the church's presence in the city and laid the groundwork for its future growth and influence. Their ministries and legacies continue to inspire and shape Christian communities worldwide, reminding us of the transformative power of faith, the resilience of the human spirit, and the enduring message of love and hope that Christianity represents.

The impact of Peter and Paul on the development of the Roman church can be seen in several key areas:

Theology:
Both Peter and Paul contributed significantly to the development of early Christian theology. Peter's writings, particularly his first epistle, focused on the nature of faith, the importance of Christian living, and the need for perseverance in the face of persecution. Paul's writings, including his letters to the Romans, Corinthians, and Galatians explored the relationship between faith and works, the nature of grace, and the universal availability of salvation.

Church organization:
The ministries of Peter and Paul played a crucial role in establishing the organizational structures of the early church in Rome. They likely played a key role in establishing leadership roles within the church, including bishops, presbyters, and deacons. Their teachings and leadership contributed to the development of a hierarchical structure within the Roman church, which would become a defining characteristic of Christian organization in the centuries to come.

Missionary activity:
Both Peter and Paul were active missionaries, spreading the Gospel message to diverse communities in Rome and beyond. They actively sought to reach both Jewish and Gentile audiences, emphasizing the universality of the Christian message and the possibility of salvation for all who accepted Christ. Their missionary endeavors contributed to the rapid expansion of Christianity within the Roman Empire and beyond.

Theological debates:
Both figures actively engaged in theological debates within the Roman church and beyond. Peter's writings, including his first epistle, addressed concerns

related to the role of Jewish law in Christian life and the growing tensions between Jewish and Gentile Christians. Paul's writings, particularly his letters to the Romans and Galatians, addressed issues like the relationship between faith and works, the law's role, and Gentiles' inclusivity within the Christian community. These debates contributed to the development of early Christian theology and the formation of various Christian traditions.

While brief, the ministries of Peter and Paul in Rome had a profound impact on the development of the Roman church. They established a foundation for the church's growth, shaped its theological outlook, and contributed to its organizational structure. Their martyrdom, symbolizing their unwavering faith and the resilience of the early church, inspired countless Christians in the centuries to come. Their legacies continue to inspire and guide Christian communities worldwide, reminding us of the enduring power of faith and the transformative message of Christianity.

23. THE ROMAN PERSECUTIONS AND THEIR IMPACT

With its vast expanse and complex social structure, the Roman Empire presented opportunities and challenges for the nascent Christian movement. While some Romans were drawn to the message of love, forgiveness, and equality espoused by Jesus, others viewed Christianity as a subversive force, a threat to the established order. The early years of the Christian faith in Rome were marked by periods of both remarkable growth and intense persecution.

The arrival of Christianity in Rome is often attributed to the Apostle Peter, who is traditionally believed to have established the first church there around the middle of the first century. The apostle Paul, known for his missionary journeys and writings, also played a significant role in developing the Christian community in Rome. His letters, written during the mid-first century, provide valuable insights into the lives and challenges of early Christians in the city.

Several factors fueled the growth of Christianity in Rome. The city's diverse population, including many Jews and foreigners, provided fertile ground for spreading the Gospel message. Early Christians in Rome, drawn by the message of hope and community found in the teachings of Jesus, formed small, tightly knit groups, often gathering in private homes for worship, prayer, and mutual support. They shared their faith with friends and family members and neighbors, gradually expanding influence throughout the city.

However, alongside this growth, the early Christians faced a significant obstacle: the Roman Empire's official religion centered on worshipping the emperor and the gods of the Roman pantheon. Christians who refused to participate in these rituals and who worshipped only one God were seen as a threat to the empire's stability and unity. They were accused of atheism and disloyalty and faced suspicion and hostility by many Romans.

The first documented persecutions of Christians in Rome occurred during the reign of the emperor Nero in 64 AD. Following a massive fire that ravaged the city, Nero sought to deflect blame and scapegoat the Christian community. He accused Christians of setting the fire, a charge they vehemently denied and launched a wave of persecution. Christians were subjected to torture, public executions, and gruesome deaths, often being thrown to wild animals in the Colosseum or burned alive. This persecution solidified the image of Christians as enemies of the state, and it had a profound impact on the church's development.

Despite their challenges, early Christians in Rome remained steadfast in their faith. They found solace and strength in their shared beliefs, and they were inspired by the example of their martyrs, who willingly gave their lives for their convictions. Their resilience and unwavering devotion in the face of adversity served as a powerful testament to the enduring power of their faith.

The persecutions continued sporadically under subsequent emperors, with varying degrees of intensity. Emperor Domitian, during his reign in the late first century, launched a campaign of persecution against Christians, targeting prominent church leaders and subjecting them to imprisonment and execution. The reign of Emperor Trajan in the early second century marked a turning point, as he introduced a policy of officially tolerating Christianity, even though it was still considered an illegal religion.

The persecution of Christians in Rome reached its peak during the reign of Emperor Decius in the mid-third century. Decius issued an edict requiring all citizens to offer sacrifices to the Roman gods and to obtain a certificate of sacrifice. Christians who refused to comply were subjected to imprisonment, torture, and death. This persecution was particularly severe, and it forced many Christians to make difficult choices. Some chose to renounce their faith and obtain the certificate, while others remained steadfast, enduring hardship and persecution.

However, the church endured and even thrived during these turbulent times. The persecutions, while tragic, also served to strengthen the Christian community. They fostered a sense of solidarity and commitment as Christians drew closer to one another and supported each other in the face of adversity. Christians' martyrdom became a powerful symbol of their faith and conviction, inspiring others to persevere and remain true to their beliefs.

The persecutions also significantly impacted the development of Christian theology and practice. The experience of suffering and persecution led to the development of a theology of martyrdom, which viewed the death of Christians as a victory over evil and a testament to the power of faith. The practice of prayer and communal support flourished during times of persecution, as Christians found strength and encouragement in one another. The persecution also led to the development of a sense of Christian identity that was distinct from the surrounding Roman culture, as Christians sought to maintain their faith and values in a hostile world.

Despite facing the challenges of persecution, the early church in Rome grew and flourished, establishing itself as a center of Christian faith and influence. The commitment of early Christians, their unwavering faith, and the examples of their martyrs left an enduring legacy, shaping the development of Christianity and its impact on the world.

24. THE DEVELOPMENT OF ROMAN CHURCH ORGANIZATION AND HIERARCHY

Like a seed planted in fertile ground, the early church in Rome took root and flourished. The city, a bustling center of commerce and culture, provided a fertile ground for the Gospel message to spread. This expansion was further catalyzed by the presence of key figures like Peter and Paul, who, through their ministry, shaped the spiritual landscape of the city.

Peter, revered as the "rock" upon which Jesus built his church, is believed to have established a community of believers in Rome. While the precise date of his arrival remains debated, his presence in the city is attested to by early Christian writers. Tradition holds that Peter was martyred in Rome during the reign of Nero, his execution mirroring the crucifixion of Jesus. This event, though steeped in tragedy, served as a powerful symbol of the church's commitment to its faith, even in the face of persecution.

Paul, a former persecutor of Christians who underwent a dramatic conversion experience on the road to Damascus, played a significant role in the growth of Christianity in Rome. His letters, notably the epistle to the Romans, attest to the thriving community of believers in the city, a testament to the power of his message and his unwavering commitment to spreading the Gospel. Paul's own martyrdom in Rome, sometime between 64 and 67 AD, further solidified the city's importance in the early Christian world.

These figures and others who arrived in Rome during this formative period laid the foundation for the church's growth and development. Though facing challenges and opposition, the early Christian communities in Rome persevered. They met in homes, sharing the Gospel message, celebrating the

Lord's Supper, and supporting one another. Their commitment to faith and community laid the groundwork for the church's future evolution.

As the church in Rome grew, so did the need for organization and structure. This led to the emergence of a hierarchical system, with distinct roles and responsibilities assigned to various individuals within the church. The development of this hierarchical structure, though seemingly a natural progression, was a complex process influenced by factors like the city's size, the increasing number of believers, and the desire for order and stability.

At the church's helm stood the bishop, whose role evolved over time from being a local community leader to a figure with increasing authority and responsibility. The bishop, often referred to as the"overseer, " held primary responsibility for the community's spiritual well-being, offering guidance, teaching, and oversight. The bishop's authority, however, was not absolute, as he was expected to consult with the community and seek their input in decision-making.

Presbyters, or elders, supported the bishop, who played an integral role in the church's governance and spiritual leadership. The presbyters, often chosen from among the community's respected members, served as advisors to the bishop, assisting in the administration of the church and providing spiritual guidance to the congregation.

The third tier in this evolving structure comprised deacons, individuals tasked with serving the church's and its members' practical needs. These individuals were often responsible for tasks such as caring for the poor and sick,distributing alms, and managing the church's finances. Their role emphasized the importance of practical service and compassion in the early church.

The emergence of this hierarchical structure, while providing organization and stability, was not without its complexities. Some early Christians, particularly those with a Jewish background, viewed the development of a hierarchical system with suspicion. They feared that such an organization might detract from the essential equality of all believers before God.

This tension between the desire for order and the emphasis on equality is a recurring theme in the church's history, a reminder of the constant need to balance structure with the individual's spiritual needs. However, the development of a hierarchical structure was instrumental in the church's continued growth and expansion. It allowed the church to effectively govern its affairs, respond to the needs of its expanding community, and continue spreading the Gospel message across the Roman Empire and beyond.

As the church in Rome continued to flourish, it became a hub of theological development, attracting scholars and thinkers who sought to understand the complexities of the Christian faith. This period witnessed the emergence of significant theological figures like Justin Martyr, Clement of Alexandria, and Origen, whose writings provided insights into the early church's understanding of God, the nature of Christ, and the relationship between faith and reason. These thinkers, drawing upon the wisdom of Greek philosophy and engaging with the cultural landscape of their time, contributed to the intellectual and spiritual vibrancy of the Roman church.

The early church in Rome, a testament to the power of faith and community, emerged as a beacon of light in a complexand often challenging world. Its growth, shaped by the ministries of prominent figures, the development of organizational structure, and the intellectual contributions of theological giants, set the stage for the church's future trajectory. This period, marked by both triumph and adversity serves as a reminder of the church's enduring spirit and its transformative influence on the world.

The Significance of Rome in Early Christianity

Rome, the Eternal City, played a pivotal role in the unfolding story of early Christianity, shaping the faith's trajectory and leaving an indelible mark on its development. Its influence extended far beyond the confines of the Roman Empire, impacting the church's growth, organization, and theology for centuries to come. The confluence of factors that made Rome a fertile ground for Christianity was a complex interplay of historical circumstances, cultural trends, and the unwavering dedication of early Christian missionaries.

The city's immense size and global reach as the capital of the Roman Empire served as a powerful magnet for people from across the known world. Its teeming population, drawn to the promise of prosperity and opportunity, included diverse individuals seeking new beginnings, a new faith, or simply a new life. This melting pot of cultures and ideologies provided a fertile ground for the Gospel message to take root and spread.

The city's bustling port, a vital hub for trade and communication facilitated the movement of people and ideas. Merchants, travelers, and soldiers carried with them the seeds of the Christian faith, spreading it along the arteries of the Roman Empire and beyond. The Roman road system, a testament to the empire's engineering prowess, provided efficient pathways for Christian missionaries to disseminate the Gospel message far and wide.

The influence of prominent figures like Peter and Paul, both martyred in Rome, further solidified the city's position as a center of Christian influence. Peter was considered the "rock" upon which the church was built, and Paul, the apostle to the Gentiles, played crucial roles in establishing and nurturing the Christian community in Rome. Their ministries, characterized by fervent preaching, powerful testimonies, and unwavering commitment to the faith, attracted many followers, including influential individuals who contributed to the church's expansion.

The early Christian communities in Rome faced formidable challenges. At its peak, the Roman Empire adhered to a polytheistic system of worship, viewing Christianity as a threat to its established religious and social order. This led to periods of persecution, where Christians were subjected to imprisonment, torture, and even execution for their beliefs.

However, the Roman persecutions, while harrowing, served as a catalyst for the church's growth. Faced with adversity, Christians found strength in their faith, demonstrating unwavering resilience and unwavering loyalty to their convictions. Their willingness to endure suffering for the sake of the Gospel message inspired many, solidifying the church's position as a vibrant and growing force in the Roman world.

The experiences of the early Roman church, shaped by persecution, resilience, and a deep commitment to the faith, profoundly impacted the development of Christian theology and doctrine. Early Christians in Rome engaged in passionate debates about the nature of Christ, the role of the Trinity, and the interpretation of scripture.

While sometimes contentious, these debates contributed to a more nuanced and sophisticated understanding of Christian beliefs. This process of theological exploration laid the foundation for the development of the church's creed, its foundational statements of faith, and its evolving understanding of the Gospel message.

Rome's influence extended far beyond theological discourse. The city's role as the heart of the Roman Empire shaped the organization and governance of the early church. Early Christians, often persecuted and facing challenging circumstances, recognized the need for structure and organization. This need led to the emergence of bishops, presbyters, and deacons, who served as leaders within the Roman church, guiding and supporting the growing Christian community.

The development of a hierarchical structure within the Roman church, with the bishop of Rome assuming a prominent leadership role, contributed to the eventual rise of the papacy. While the papacy's evolution would take

centuries, the early Roman church's organizational structure laid the foundation for this significant development.

Rome's legacy in the history of Christianity extends far beyond its role as a center of theological and organizational development. The city profoundly influenced Christian art, architecture, and culture. Despite facing persecution, the early Christians in Rome actively engaged with the artistic and architectural traditions of the Roman Empire. They adopted elements of Roman design in constructing churches, utilizing the grandeur and beauty of Roman architecture to create spaces that fostered Christian worship and community. This fusion of Christian symbolism and Roman artistic tradition paved the way for a distinct Christian art and architecture would leave an enduring mark on the world.

The influence of Rome's cultural and social norms on Christian practices were significant. As Christianity gained momentum within the Roman Empire, it encountered and adapted to the prevailing social customs and traditions. This process of cultural interaction led to the adoption of Roman elements, like the use of Latin as the primary language of the church, the incorporation of Roman liturgical practices, and the integration of Christian values into Roman social structures.

While the Roman Empire's influence on the development of early Christianity was significant, it was not without its challenges. The early Christians in Rome faced cultural tensions as they navigated the complexities of living as Christians in a pagan world. They grappled with issues like idolatry, societal expectations, and the tension between Christian values and Roman practices.

Despite these challenges, the Roman church's unwavering commitment to the Gospel message, resilience in the face of persecution, and willingness to engage with the broader cultural landscape enabled it to emerge as a powerful and influential force in the Roman world. The church's growth and the gradual shift in the relationship between Christianity and the Roman Empire marked a pivotal moment in the history of faith.

The story of early Christianity in Rome is a compelling testament to the power of faith, resilience, and the enduring influence of a city that shaped the course of the Christian faith for centuries to come. The city's legacy continues to reverberate through the church's history, its impact visible in the church's organization, its theological development, and its enduring presence in the world. As we explore the rich tapestry of early Christianity, understanding the significance of Rome's role in shaping the faith's journey allows us to appreciate the transformative power of the Gospel message and the enduring legacy of a city that stood at the heart of its early development.

25. THE NATURE AND CAUSES OF EARLY CHRISTIAN HERESIES

The early Christian church was a dynamic and rapidly evolving entity, grappling with diverse theological interpretations and grappling with the influence of external forces. As Christianity spread beyond its Jewish roots and into a wider world, new ideas and interpretations of Jesus' teachings emerged. These interpretations, often diverging significantly from the established doctrines, came to be known as heresies.

Heresy, in its simplest definition, refers to a belief or doctrine that contradicts the accepted teachings of a religious community. In early Christianity, these disagreements were often deeply rooted in the attempts to reconcile Jesus' teachings with the existing Jewish faith and the prevailing philosophical currents of the Roman world. The emergence of these heresies was a testament to the early church's vibrant and often tumultuous intellectual landscape.

Theological Foundations of Early Christian Heresies:

One of the most prominent themes in early Christian heresies was the nature of Jesus Christ. While most Christians affirmed his divinity, some questioned his relationship with God the Father. For instance, the Gnostics, a diverse group of early Christians, believed that Jesus was a divine being who had descended to Earth to impart secret knowledge, or "gnosis," to those who were chosen. They viewed the physical world as a realm of illusion and believed that the material body was inherently evil. Their teachings often emphasized the importance of spiritual enlightenment and the rejection of material possessions.

Another significant heresy was Arianism, named after its founder, Arius. Arianism challenged the orthodox view of the Trinity, asserting that Jesus was not equal to God the Father but rather a created being, albeit a superior one. This dispute centered around the concept of Christ's divine nature and relationship with the Father. Arianism gained considerable support in the fourth century, leading to significant theological debates and eventually to the Council of Nicaea in 325 AD.

Other heresies focused on the nature of salvation. The Docetists, for example, believed that Jesus only appeared to be human, claiming that his physical body was an illusion and that his death and resurrection were merely appearances. Their teachings emphasized the separation of the divine from the material and challenged the traditional understanding of Christ's incarnation. They believed that salvation came through knowledge, not through faith and action, further distancing themselves from the mainstream Christian doctrines.

The Appeal of Heresies

The emergence of these diverse heresies, though often deemed heretical by the established church, reflects the ongoing search for understanding and meaning within the nascent Christian faith. They were attractive to some because they offered alternative interpretations of complex theological issues. Gnosticism, for instance, appealed to those who sought a more mystical and esoteric understanding of Christianity. Arianism attracted some who found the concept of a divine Son inferior to the Father more intellectually appealing than the orthodox doctrine of the Trinity. These heresies also offered comfort and hope in a world facing political turmoil, social upheaval, and existential anxieties.

The appeal of these alternative interpretations highlights the complex relationship between faith and reason, between spiritual intuition and intellectual inquiry, within the early Christian church. While the mainstream church sought to define a clear and coherent set of doctrines, the diversity of theological interpretations underscored the ongoing struggle to reconcile faith with reason, the spiritual with the intellectual.

Impact of Heresies on the Early Church:
The emergence of these heresies had a profound impact on the early church. They sparked heated debates, leading to theological disputes and sometimes even persecution. The controversies over the nature of Christ and the relationship between the Father and the Son, as seen in Arianism, created divisions within the church, forcing it to confront internal conflicts and define its core doctrines. The church's response to these heresies shaped its evolution and ultimately led to the development of a more structured and defined theological system.

Furthermore, attempts to define orthodoxy and combat heresy led to the emergence of church councils. These gatherings of bishops and theologians were called to address pressing theological issues and establish a consensus on Christian doctrine. The Council of Nicea, convened in 325 AD by Emperor Constantine, was a landmark event that resulted in the formulation of the Nicene Creed, which became a cornerstone of Christian faith and continues to be a fundamental statement of belief for many Christian denominations. The church councils played a crucial role in shaping the direction of the church, solidifying its core doctrines, and establishing a more unified theological framework. Though the early church faced challenges from within and without, its efforts to define its theological foundations and respond to the challenges of heresy laid the groundwork for the future development of Christianity. The legacy of this period of intense theological debate and doctrinal clarification continues to resonate within the diverse denominations of Christianity today.

The Nature of Heresy: Defining Orthodoxy

The emergence of heresy posed a significant challenge to the early church. It forced them to confront the question of what it meant to be a true Christian and to articulate a definitive set of beliefs that could be considered orthodox. While the early church valued diversity of thought and expression, it also recognized the need to preserve Jesus's core teachings and establish a foundational framework for its faith.

In response to the challenge of heresy, the church sought to define its essential beliefs through the process of canonization, the selection and establishment of authoritative texts. This process was not a simple or immediate one but rather a gradual evolution over several centuries.

The church gradually compiled and canonized the New Testament scriptures, which served as the foundation for Christian theology and interpretation. This process also included rejecting texts that were considered heretical, which further solidified the church's doctrinal boundaries. The process of canonization was closely intertwined with the development of ecclesiastical authority. As the church grew and spread, it became increasingly necessary to establish a hierarchy of leadership and to develop mechanisms for resolving theological disputes. The emergence of bishops, presbyters, and deacons, as well as the establishment of church councils, were key steps in this process. These institutions provided a framework for maintaining order, promoting doctrine uniformity, and addressing heresy challenges.

The Impact of Heresy on Christian Doctrine:

Despite the challenges presented by heresy, it played a crucial role in shaping the development of Christian doctrine. By forcing the church to engage in rigorous debate and to clarify its core beliefs, heresy served as a catalyst for theological growth and refinement. The controversies surrounding Arianism,

Docetism, and other heresies led to the formulation of definitive statements of faith, such as the Nicene Creed, which are essential expressions of Christian belief today. These debates also fostered a deeper understanding of the scriptures and the relationship between faith and reason, shaping the intellectual landscape of the early church.

It's crucial to understand that the designation of a belief as "heretical" was often determined by those in positions of authority within the church. This raises complex questions about the nature of orthodoxy and the potential for power dynamics to influence the definition of truth. The history of early Christian heresies underscores the ongoing tension between seeking truth and maintaining unity between intellectual inquiry and ecclesiastical authority.

Beyond the Heresy:

The story of early Christian heresies is not merely a catalog of theological disputes. It is also a powerful testament to the human search for meaning, understanding, and faith. These heresies reveal the diversity of perspectives that emerged as Christianity spread beyond its Jewish origins and encountered the complexities of the Roman world. The intellectual and spiritual energy that drove these debates ultimately contributed to developing a rich and diverse Christian tradition.

The early church's struggle with heresy was a defining moment in its history, shaping its theology, organization, and identity. By wrestling with these challenges, the church emerged stronger, its core doctrines more clearly defined, and its mission more clearly focused. The legacy of these debates continues to resonate within the diverse Christian communities of today, reminding us of the ongoing search for understanding and meaning within the context of faith.

26. THE SIGNIFICANCE OF EARLY CHURCH COUNCILS

The emergence of Christianity, with its rapid expansion and adoption by diverse populations, brought about many challenges. Chief among these was the need to address the growing diversity of beliefs and practices within the nascent Christian community. This diversity, while reflective of the universality of the Gospel message, also presented a potential source of division and conflict. As the Christian faith spread beyond its Jewish origins, it encountered new cultures, philosophies, and interpretations of the message of Jesus. This led to a burgeoning of diverse perspectives on fundamental theological questions, giving rise to the phenomenon of heresy.

Heresy, in its simplest definition, refers to beliefs or practices that deviate from the accepted doctrines of a religious community. Within the early Christian church, heresies emerged from a confluence of factors, including the interpretation of scripture, the nature of Jesus Christ, the relationship between God and humanity, and the church's authority. These controversies challenged the nascent Christian community's unity and posed a threat to the core tenets of their faith.

In this context, the early church councils, held in various cities across the Roman Empire, played a pivotal role in shaping the trajectory of Christian doctrine. These councils, gatherings of church leaders and theologians, aimed to address theological controversies, establish consensus on key beliefs, and define the boundaries of acceptable Christian thought. The councils were not simply gatherings for debate but also represented a significant step towards institutionalizing and organizing the Christian faith.

One of the most significant early councils was the The Council of Jerusalem was held around 50 CE. This council addressed the question of whether gentile converts to Christianity needed to adhere to Jewish law, particularly circumcision. The council's decision, documented in Acts 15, was a crucial step in affirming the universal reach of the Gospel and recognizing the equal standing of both Jewish and gentile believers within the Christian community. This decision helped pave the way for Christianity's broader acceptance and spread throughout the Roman Empire.

However, the Council of Jerusalem was just beginning. As the church expanded, other controversies arose, demanding further dialogue and resolution. One of the most significant of these was the Arian controversy, named after the theologian Arius. Arius challenged the orthodox understanding of the nature of Christ, arguing that Jesus was not truly divine but a created being, subordinate to God the Father. This controversy, which raged for decades, threatened to fracture the Christian church, sparking intense debates and theological battles.

The Council of Nicea, convened in 325 CE by the Roman Emperor Constantine, aimed to address the Arian controversy and restore unity to the Christian world. This council, a landmark event in Christian history, brought together bishops from across the empire for a series of heated deliberations. After months of intense discussion, the council ultimately condemned Arianism and affirmed the orthodox belief in the divinity of Christ, declaring that Jesus was "God from God, Light from Light, true God from true God." This affirmation, enshrined in the Nicene Creed, became a cornerstone of Christian theology, defining the nature of the Trinity and the relationship between Father, Son, and Holy Spirit.

The Council of Nicea was a model for future councils, establishing a precedent for addressing theological disputes through reasoned debate and consensus-building. It also demonstrated the growing influence of the

Roman Empire in shaping the direction of Christianity as the emperor's involvement signaled the growing political significance of the Christian church.

The significance of these early church councils cannot be overstated. They were crucial in shaping the core doctrines of Christianity, establishing a foundation for Christian theology, and defining the boundaries of acceptable belief within the church. Their decisions, often reached after protracted debates and disagreements, solidified key tenets of faith, including the nature of Christ, the relationship between God and humanity, and the role of scripture.

Furthermore, the councils played a vital role in unifying the diverse Christian communities, resolving theological controversies, and fostering a sense of shared identity and purpose. Establishing a framework for doctrinal consensus and defining the parameters of acceptable belief helped prevent fragmentation and fostered a sense of unity within the burgeoning Christian world.

The impact of these early councils is evident in the enduring influence of the Nicene Creed, a foundational statement of Christian faith that continues to be recited in churches worldwide. Though debated and contested throughout history, their decisions established a framework for theological discourse that continues to shape Christian thought and practice today.

The legacy of the early church councils is not simply one of doctrinal definition but also one of demonstrating the importance of dialogue, debate, and consensus-building in addressing theological controversies. These gatheringsserved as a model for subsequent councils, laying the groundwork for the ongoing process of theological reflection, interpretation, and development within the Christian church.

The early church councils stand as a testament to the dynamism of early Christianity, a faith that was constantly evolving, adapting, and confronting the challenges of its time. They highlight the importance of addressing theological controversies, the need for defining core beliefs, and the power of dialogue and consensus-building in shaping a shared faith. While rooted in the historical context of the early Christian church, these councils continue to offer valuable insights into the ongoing process of theological inquiry, the importance of unity in the face of diversity, and the enduring legacy of the Christian faith.

The Council of Nicea and the Definition of the Trinity The year 325 AD marked a pivotal moment in the history of Christianity. The Roman Emperor Constantine, having embraced the Christian faith and recognizing the church's growing influence, convened a council in the city of Nicea, located in modern-day Turkey. This gathering, known as the Council of Nicea, was not merely a meeting of church leaders but a defining moment in the development of Christian doctrine and the shaping of the Christian faith.

The council's primary objective was to address a theological controversy that had been brewing within the church for several years. The central issue at stake was the nature of Christ—his relationship to God the Father. Arius, a presbyter from Alexandria, had put forward a doctrine that challenged the traditional understanding of Christ's divinity. Arius argued that Christ was not truly God but rather a created being, subordinate to God the Father. This view, known as Arianism, caused widespread controversy and threatened to divide the church.

The Council of Nicea brought together bishops from across the Roman Empire, representing diverse theological perspectives. The deliberations were intense, marked by passionate arguments and fervent debates. The bishops grappled with the complexities of reconciling the divinity of Christ with his humanity, seeking to articulate a coherent and unified understanding of his nature.

After weeks of intense discussion, the council reached a consensus, condemning Arianism and defining the orthodox position on the nature of Christ. This landmark decision was codified in the Nicene Creed, a statement of faith that became a cornerstone of Christian theology. The creed affirmed the divinity of Christ, declaring that he was "begotten, not made, being of one Being with the Father." This declaration, known as the doctrine of the Trinity, became a fundamental principle of Christian belief, asserting that God exists as three persons—Father, Son, and Holy Spirit—who are distinct but co-equal.

The Council of Nicea's work went beyond simply condemning Arianism. It established a framework for the church's ongoing development and its role in the Roman Empire. By assembling bishops from various regions, the council recognized the importance of unity and consensus within the church. The Nicene Creed became a unifying force, establishing a common ground for diverse Christian communities and providing a foundation for future theological discussions.

The council's decision had far-reaching implications. It solidified the doctrine of the Trinity, which would shape Christian theology and spirituality for centuries to come. It also marked a turning point in the relationship between Christianity and the Roman Empire. Constantine signaled his support for the Christian faith and its growing influence by endorsing the Nicene Creed.

However, the Council of Nicea did not eliminate theological disputes. Arianism persisted, even though it was condemned by the council. The Arian controversy continued to divide the church for several decades, leading to further councils and ongoing debates. But despite these challenges, the Council of Nicea is a testament to the church's commitment to theological clarity and unity.

The Nicene Creed remains a powerful symbol of the church's faith, a reminder of the debates and struggles that shaped Christian belief. It continues to be recited in Christian churches worldwide, a testament to the enduring legacy of the Council of Nicea and its pivotal role in defining the foundations of the Christian faith.

The Council of Nicea's work did not end with the formulation of the Nicene Creed. It also established a model for future church councils, setting a precedent for gatherings of bishops to address theological controversies, define doctrine, and strengthen the church's unity. In the following decades, numerous other councils were convened, each addressing specific theological disputes and contributing to the evolving landscape of Christian thought.

The Council of Nicea, with its affirmation of the Trinity, played a crucial role in shaping the development of Christian theology and the emergence of the church as a major force in the Roman Empire. Its legacy continues to resonate in the hearts and minds of Christians today, reminding us of the ongoing journey of faith, the challenges of theological discourse, and the power of unity in the face of diversity.

The Arian Controversy and its Impact

The Arian controversy, a major theological dispute that rocked the early church, centered on the nature of Christ. It was a battle between two opposing interpretations of the relationship between Jesus and God the Father. The controversy emerged around the teachings of Arius, a priest from Alexandria, who argued that Jesus was not divine but a created being, subordinate to God the Father.

Arius's teachings, which were embraced by many, challenged the prevailing view that Jesus was fully divine, part of the Trinity, and equal in substance to God the Father. Arius asserted that the Father created the Son, making him a lesser being than God the Father. He claimed that the Son was "like" God but not "of the same substance" (homoousios) as God. This theological divergence sparked a fierce debate within the Christian community, dividing churches and leading to years of heated arguments and political maneuvering.

The controversy quickly spread beyond Alexandria, reaching the heart of the Roman Empire. In 325 AD, Emperor Constantine, seeking to unify the empire under a single Christian faith, convened the Council of Nicea to resolve this theological dispute. The council, composed of bishops from across the empire, ultimately condemned Arius' teachings, affirming that Jesus was "God from God, Light from Light, true God from true God, begotten, not made, of one Being with the Father."

The Council of Nicea's decision, which gave rise to the Nicene Creed, became a pivotal moment in the history of Christianity. It established the doctrine of the Trinity—thebelief that God exists as a unity of the Father, the Son, and the Holy Spirit. This doctrine, affirmed by the Council of Nicea, became a cornerstone of Christian faith, shaping theological and devotional practices for centuries to come.

The controversy, however, did not end with the Council of Nicea. Arianism continued to have a significant impact on the development of Christian thought and the political landscape of the Roman Empire. Arianism, though condemned, found support among various political and social groups, leading to further disputes and divisions within the church.

The Arian controversy's legacy extended beyond its immediate impact on the early church. It underscores the power of theological debates to shape the course of religious history. The controversy highlighted the importance of establishing clear doctrinal statements, the influence of political power on religious matters, and the challenges of reconciling diverse theological interpretations.

The Arian controversy also illuminates the enduring importance of understanding Christ's nature. It reminds us that the question of Jesus' identity, whether as a human being, a divine being, or a combination of both, continues to be a significant theological question that has generated debate and discussion throughout Christian history.

The Arian controversy also profoundly impacted the development of Christian thought and the evolution of the Church. It led to the formation of distinct theological schools contributed to the growth of monasticism as a means of preserving and propagating orthodox theology and influenced the development of the Church's hierarchical structure.

One significant development was the emergence of strong theological leaders who defended the orthodox position against Arianism. Figures like Athanasius of Alexandria, a staunch defender of the Nicene Creed, played a vital role in combating Arianism and solidifying the orthodox view of Christ. Athanasius, a scholar and theologian, wrote extensively to defend Christ's true nature and expose the errors of Arianism. He endured exile and persecution for his unwavering commitment to the Orthodox faith, ultimately becoming a martyr for the cause.

The Arian controversy also fueled the development of monasticism. Monasteries often seen as havens of intellectual and spiritual life became centers for preserving and transmitting orthodox theology. Monks, dedicated to a life of prayer and study, played a crucial role in promoting the Nicene Creed and challenging the influence of Arianism. They wrote commentaries on scripture, engaged in theological debates, and copied ancient texts, ensuring the continuity of orthodox teachings.

The controversy also contributed to the strengthening of the Church's hierarchy. The Council of Nicea, and the subsequent theological debates, highlighted the need for greater clarity and consistency in matters of doctrine. The Church, in response, saw a rise in the authority of bishops and the emergence of a more defined hierarchical structure to ensure theological uniformity and guard against the spread of heresy.

Though initially a challenge to the developing Christian faith, the Arian controversy ultimately helped solidify its core doctrines and shape its organizational structure. It demonstrated the importance of maintaining a unified theological vision and the need to address controversies through dialogue and debate. Though the Arian controversy represents a period of internal struggle, it ultimately contributed to the growth and maturity of the Christian faith, paving the way for the Church's continued development and influence throughout history.

The Evolution of Church Authority and Governance
The rise of heresy and the convening of early Church councils were responses to theological controversies and catalysts for the evolution of church authority and governance. As the Christian community expanded beyond its initial Jewish roots, it faced the challenge of defining its identity amidst a spectrum of beliefs and practices. The need for unity and clarity prompted the emergence of influential leaders and the development of structures that would shape the church's future. Early Christians often considered the Apostles, particularly Peter and Paul, exemplars of faith and authority. Their teachings and actions were viewed as authoritative sources for understanding and interpreting Jesus' message. This reverence for apostolic tradition laid the foundation for developing a leadership structure within the church. The term "apostle" itself, signifying a special commission from Jesus, carried immense weight, even as the original Apostles' lives drew to a close.

The need for leadership and guidance in growing communities led to the emergence of local church leaders known as bishops, elders (presbyters), and deacons. These individuals held positions of responsibility within their communities, providing spiritual leadership, overseeing church affairs, and mediating disputes. The bishops, particularly in major cities like Rome,

Alexandria, and Antioch, gradually gained prominence as the church expanded geographically.

The increasing influence of bishops can be attributed to several factors. As centers of Christian activity, major cities naturally became hubs of church life. The bishops in these cities often assumed the role of coordinating and overseeing smaller churches in surrounding regions. This practice, coupled with their proximity to prominent early Christians and their access to important resources, contributed to the growth of their authority.

The rise of heresies further propelled the development of church governance structures. Divergent interpretations of Christian doctrine and practice, particularly regarding the nature of Jesus Christ, challenged the unity of the church. The need for clear doctrinal definitions and establishing a system for resolving disputes led to the convening of church councils. The Council of Jerusalem held around 50 CE, marked a significant moment in early church governance. It addressed the issue of whether Gentile converts needed to follow Jewish customs. The council's decision, recorded in the Book of Acts, emphasized the importance of faith in Jesus Christ over adherence to Jewish law. This event served as a precedent for future councils, demonstrating the church's ability to address theological controversies and establish guidelines for its members.

The most famous early council, the Council of Nicea, convened in 325 CE, is a pivotal example of the church's evolving authority. Summoned by the Roman Emperor Constantine, the council aimed to resolve the Arian controversy, a major theological dispute regarding Jesus' divinity. The council's deliberations, involving bishops from across the Roman Empire, led to the creation of the Nicene Creed, a foundational statement of Christian belief that affirmed Jesus' divinity and established the doctrine of the Trinity.

The Nicene Council's significance goes beyond its specific theological pronouncements. It solidified the role of bishops as authoritative figures in the church and established a precedent for the church to address theological controversies through conciliar gatherings. The council's decisions, backed by the Roman Emperor, provided a framework for settling doctrinal disputes and maintaining unity amidst diversity. The evolution of church authority and governance in this period was a complex process, shaped by a confluence of factors, including apostolic tradition, the growth of local church leadership, the rise of heresies, and the influence of the Roman Empire. The emergence of bishops as prominent figures, the development of conciliar gatherings, and the establishment of doctrinal statements marked a turning point in the church's organization and its capacity to manage its growing complexity. While these developments ushered in a new era of church governance, they also laid the foundation for future theological and political struggles, demonstrating the enduring interplay between faith, authority, and power in shaping the Christian tradition.

27. THE IMPACT OF ROMAN LAW AND ADMINISTRATION:

With its vast legal system and intricate administrative apparatus, the Roman Empire cast a long shadow over the burgeoning Christian movement. This influence was profound and multifaceted, shaping the organization, practices, and identity of early Christian communities.

While the Romans viewed Christianity with a mixture of suspicion and curiosity, the legal status of Christians was often precarious, fluctuating between periods of relative tolerance and outright persecution. The evolving relationship between the church and the state would become a defining feature of early Christianity, leaving an enduring mark on the development of the faith.

The Roman legal framework, a complex system of written laws, precedents, and judicial procedures, provided a context for the burgeoning Christian communities. Roman law offered a degree of clarity and structure, albeit within a system that was often ambiguous in its application to religious groups like the early Christians. Christians initially faced challenges in navigating the complexities of Roman law, particularly in areas such as property ownership, inheritance, and the administration of religious affairs.

Roman law, emphasizing civic duty, loyalty to the state, and respect for traditional deities, presented a tension with Christian beliefs, especially those related to the supremacy of Christ and the rejection of idolatry. This tension would lead to periods of persecution and conflict, where Christian communities often found themselves at odds with the Roman legal system.

The administration of the Roman Empire, a vast network of officials, institutions, and systems, also significantly impacted early Christianity. Roman administrative practices influenced the organization and functioning of Christian communities. For example, the Roman model of centralized governance and hierarchical structures, with emperors and officials wielding authority, found parallels in the early Christian church's development of its own hierarchy, with bishops, presbyters, and deacons assuming leadership positions.

The Roman system of communication and infrastructure facilitated the spread of the Christian message, allowing early Christians to connect with one another and share their faith across vast distances. Roman roads, postal systems, and public gathering spaces provided avenues for Christian communities to meet, share their beliefs, and establish networks.

However, the relationship between church and state was not without its complexities. The Roman government, while often tolerant, viewed Christianity with suspicion. It was seen as a foreign, subversive religion that challenged traditional Roman beliefs and values. The growth ofthe prominence of Christianity within the empire, particularly in urban centers, raised anxieties among Roman authorities, who saw it as a potential threat to the social order and stability of the empire. This led to periods of persecution, where Christians were targeted for their faith, often accused of sedition, undermining state authority, or refusing to participate in Roman religious rituals. These persecutions, while often sporadic and geographically limited, nevertheless profoundly impacted Christian communities, forcing them to adapt, resist, and develop strategies for survival.

The legal status of Christians within the Roman Empire was a complex and fluid matter. While they initially operated on the fringes of society, tolerated as a minor sect, the rise of Christianity and its growing popularity in the empire would lead to an evolution in their legal status. Initially, Christians were often treated with suspicion, accused of being subversive, and subject to sporadic persecution. They were frequently targeted for their refusal to participate in traditional Roman religious rituals, which often included offering sacrifices to Roman deities, a practice that contradicted their commitment to monotheistic belief in God.

The legal framework of the Roman Empire did not provide a clear definition of the legal status of Christians, leaving room for ambiguity and shifting attitudes toward them. This ambiguity allowed for both periods of relative tolerance and periods of persecution, depending on the prevailing political climate and the policies of individual emperors. The early Christians faced various challenges in navigating this legal landscape, often finding themselves caught between the desire to practice their faith and the need to avoid attracting the ire of Roman authorities.

One significant turning point in the legal status of Christians was the reign of Emperor Constantine in the 4th century. Constantine's conversion to Christianity and his subsequent support for the Christian faith marked a shift in the relationship between church and state. Christianity gained recognition and legitimacy within the Roman Empire with Constantine's backing. Constantine's famous Edict of Milan in 313 AD granted Christian's freedom of religion, ending the era of open persecution and paving the way for a more tolerant and inclusive approach toward the Christian faith.

However, even with Constantine's support, the legal status of Christians remained somewhat complex. While they enjoyed newfound freedoms, the relationship between church and state remained fluid and often entangled in matters of law, administration, and social influence. While Christianity gained prominence and influence, it continued to negotiate its place within the broader Roman legal system, shaping its structures and practices in response to the opportunities and challenges presented by the Roman legal system.

The influence of Roman law and administration on the organization and functioning of early Christian communities was profound and enduring. It shaped the development of Christian leadership, the emergence of church hierarchy, and the establishment of formal structures within the church. It also influenced the development of Christian rituals, practices and beliefs, shaping the ways in which Christians interacted with the wider Roman society.

The relationship between the church and state, marked by periods of both tolerance and persecution, ultimately contributed to the evolution of Christianity within the Roman Empire. The challenges and opportunities presented by the Roman legal system and administration forced Christians to adapt, develop strategies for survival, and ultimately contribute to the broader social and cultural landscape of the Roman world. As Christianity grew in prominence, it continued to shape the legal framework of the empire, contributing to a gradual shift in the relationship between church and state, ultimately leading to the establishment of Christianity as the dominant religion of the Roman Empire.

28.   THE ROLE OF ROMAN PATRONAGE AND SOCIAL NETWORKS

The Roman Empire provided a fertile ground for the spread of Christianity, not solely due to its vast infrastructure and Pax Romana but also through its patronage system and intricate social networks. While the Empire might have initially viewed Christianity with suspicion, its influence was crucial in fostering its growth.

Patronage, Power, and Conversion:
The Roman world was a society built on patron-client relationships. Powerful individuals, known as patrons, extended their protection and resources to those who were less fortunate, known as clients. This system permeated all aspects of Roman life, from politics to social gatherings. Within this framework, Roman elites played a pivotal role in the spread of Christianity.

Some Roman patrons were drawn to Christianity due to its message of love, compassion, and social justice. Individuals like the Roman prefect, Flavius Clemens, who converted to Christianity, offered their patronage to early Christian communities. This patronage took various forms, including financial support, legal protection, and the use of their influence within the Roman administration. Such acts of patronage not only provided resources but also facilitated the integration of Christian communities into Roman society, enhancing their legitimacy and influence.

Social Networks: A Web of Faith:
Beyond patronage, social networks played a crucial role in spreading Christianity. The early Christians often ostracized by Roman society, found solace and support within their own communities. They forged deep bonds

of fellowship, sharing their faith and offering each other spiritual guidance and material assistance.

These social networks were not limited to the lower classes. Many Christians, particularly those who had converted from the Roman elite, maintained their social connections within their former circles. This opened avenues for the Gospel to reach individuals in higher social strata. The early Christian evangelists, often former merchants or traders, used their existing networks to spread the message of Christ. They traveled far and wide, engaging with diverse populations and leveraging their connections to establish new Christian communities.

The Power of Influence:
The social connections of individuals like Paul, a Roman citizen and a skilled orator, facilitated his outreach to diverse communities. He used his knowledge of Roman law and his connections within the Roman world to navigate the complex legal and social landscape of the time. This allowed him to effectively spread the Christian message, establish churches and lay the foundation for the organized Christian church.

The Transformation of Faith:
The interaction between Christianity and the Roman Empire was a dynamic process. While the Empire initially viewed Christianity with skepticism and even persecuted its followers, the faith gradually gained traction due to the dedication of its followers, its message of hope and love, and the social connections that facilitated its spread. The Roman patronage system, while initially a source of conflict, also provided opportunities for Christian communities to gain influence and legitimacy. The social networks that early Christians established provided a strong foundation for spreading the faith, allowing the Gospel to reach diverse segments of Roman society.

The Influence of Roman Social Structures:

The impact of the Roman Empire on early Christianity was profound. The social structures and systems that characterized Roman society, including patronage and social networks, played a significant role in facilitating the spread of Christianity. This influence was not always positive, as the challenges of navigating Roman society and the threat of persecution were ever-present. However, the resilience of the early Christian communities and their willingness to embrace the Roman social fabric while maintaining their faith ultimately contributed to the rise of Christianity as a powerful force in the Roman world. The interplay between Roman patronage, social networks, and early Christian communities demonstrates the interconnected nature of history and the complex forces that shape the course of human events.

The Impact of Roman Culture on Christian Practices:

The Roman Empire was a vast and powerful civilization that profoundly influenced early Christianity's development. While the early Christians faced persecution from Roman authorities, their faith flourished within Roman culture, adopting aspects of Roman life and institutions. This section delves into the ways in which Roman culture impacted Christian practices, examining the adoption of Roman architectural styles, liturgical elements, and social customs within the emerging church.

Roman Architecture and Christian Churches:

One of the most visible ways in which Roman culture influenced Christianity was in the realm of architecture. Early Christians, initially meeting in homes and private spaces, sought larger venues for worship as their communities grew. Roman architectural forms provided a ready-made framework for their expanding needs.

The basilica, a large public building used for law courts and administrative purposes, became a favored model for early Christian churches. The basilica's rectangular shape, with a central nave flanked by aisles, provided ample space for gatherings and processions. It was well-suited for the

liturgical practices developing within the early church, allowing for clear sightlines and a sense of order.

Christian churches adopted the basilica's basic structural elements, incorporating features like vaulted ceilings, elaborate mosaics, and decorative columns. The architecture of early churches often reflected the grand scale and grandeur of Roman public buildings, a testament to the growing influence of Christianity within Roman society.

The iconic dome symbolized Roman engineering prowess and was also incorporated into Christian architecture. Early churches like the Hagia Sophia in Constantinople, built in the 6th century, showcase the magnificent fusion of Roman architectural styles and Christian symbolism.

Liturgical Practices and Roman Influence Roman culture also influenced the development of Christian liturgical practices. The early church, rooted in Jewish traditions, incorporated elements of Roman religious rituals and customs into its worship.

Incense, a common practice in Roman temples, found its way into Christian worship, symbolizing prayer and sacrifice. Hymn chanting, which originated in Roman theater, became a key aspect of Christian liturgy, adding a powerful element of music and devotion to their services.

Using candles, another borrowing from Roman religious practice, became a prominent part of Christian liturgy. Candles symbolize the light of Christ and the presence of the Holy Spirit. Bringing candles during services added a mystical and spiritual dimension to worship.

While initially drawing from Roman practice, these borrowed elements were infused with new meaning and symbolism within the Christian context. They helped shape the early church's distinctive liturgical practices and contributed to the development of a rich and evocative form of Christian worship.

Social Customs and the Christian Community:

Roman social customs also played a role in shaping the development of Christian communities. Roman society was highly hierarchical, with a strong emphasis on status and social order. While seeking to live according to their values, Christians found themselves navigating the complexities of Roman social norms.

The concept of patronage, a central feature of Roman society, where powerful individuals offered protection and support to those of lower status, was adopted and adapted by early Christians. The idea of spiritual patronage, with bishops and other church leaders serving as patrons to their flocks, became an important aspect of early church structure.

Christians also embraced the Roman practice of charity and hospitality. The early church, known for its care for the poor and marginalized, relied on the generosity of its members and the support of wealthy patrons to provide for the needs of those in need. This charitable spirit, rooted in the teachings of Jesus, reflected the Roman ideal of civic responsibility and social welfare.

The Roman emphasis on education and intellectual pursuits also influenced early Christian communities. Many early Christians, particularly those from the upper classes, were well-educated and actively engaged in theological debates and the development of Christian thought.

Challenges and Conflicts:

While Roman culture offered opportunities for the spread and growth of Christianity, it also presented significant challenges. The Roman Empire was steeped in pagan traditions and practices that clashed with Christian beliefs.

The veneration of emperors and the worship of Roman gods posed a direct challenge to Christian monotheism. Christians refusing to participate in pagan rituals faced persecution and hostility from Roman authorities.

Roman social norms also presented conflicts for early Christians. The practice of slavery, widely accepted in Roman society, was challenged by Christian teachings emphasizing the inherent dignity and equality of all human beings. This conflict created tension between Christian values and Roman customs, leading to debates and challenges within the early church.

Despite these challenges, Christianity thrived in the Roman world. Faith's adaptability, emphasis on love, compassion, and social justice, and appeal to diverse groups within Roman society contributed to its rapid growth and ultimate triumph.

Conclusion:

The Roman Empire provided fertile ground for the development of early Christianity. While facing persecution and conflicts with Roman cultural norms, Christians adopted and adapted Roman life's aspects, shaping their practices and institutions. The adoption of Roman architectural styles, liturgical elements, and social customs contributed to forming a distinct Christian identity within the context of the Roman world.

The influence of Roman culture on early Christianity was a complex and multifaceted process. It led to both challenges and opportunities, ultimately shaping the development of the Christian church and its enduring legacy. As the faith spread beyond the Roman Empire, it continued to adapt and evolve, reflecting the diverse cultural contexts in which it took root. Understanding the influence of Roman culture on early Christianity provides valuable insights into the formation of this transformative faith and its impact on the world.

29. THE CHALLENGES OF LIVING AS CHRISTIANS IN A ROMAN WORLD

The Roman Empire, with its vast expanse and complex social fabric, presented both opportunities and challenges for early Christians. Their beliefs and practices often clashed with the prevailing norms of Roman society, creating a tension that shaped the development of the Christian faith. Navigating this complex landscape required a delicate balance of adherence to their faith and accommodation to the demands of the Roman world.

One of the most significant challenges faced by early Christians were the widespread practice of idolatry within the Roman Empire. The Romans revered a pantheon of gods and goddesses whose images were prominently displayed in public spaces and private homes. They participated in various religious festivals and ceremonies dedicated to these deities, often engaging in acts of sacrifice and divination. For Christians who believed in the one true God, this practice was deeply problematic. They saw idolatry as a form of blasphemy, a betrayal of their commitment to the God who had revealed himself through Jesus Christ.

This fundamental difference in beliefs led to tensions between Christians and the Roman authorities, who saw Christianity as a subversive force. The refusal of Christians to participate in Roman religious rituals and their condemnation of idolatry was interpreted as a threat to the social order and the authority of the emperor, who was often considered a divine figure. This perception fueled sporadic periods of persecution, where Christians faced imprisonment, torture, and even death for their faith.

Another challenge arose from the Roman Empire's emphasis on social hierarchy and conformity. The Roman world was structured around a rigid system of social classes, with citizens expected to adhere to the norms and expectations associated with their particular rank. This emphasis on social order permeated all aspects of Roman life, from political participation to family relationships to religious practices.

For Christians, this social order presented a dilemma. They were taught to embrace radical equality, recognizing the inherent worth of all individuals in the eyes of God, regardless of their social status or position. This commitment to equality challenged the deeply ingrained social hierarchies of the Roman world. Christians rejected the Roman system of patronage, which required individuals to seek favor from powerful individuals and institutions. Instead, they emphasized mutual love and service, prioritizing the needs of the marginalized and those in poverty, often exceeding the limits of their own social standing.

Furthermore, the Roman world valued civic participation and loyalty to the state. Roman citizens were expected to actively engage in public life, participating in political events, serving in the military, and contributing to the empire's prosperity. This expectation clashed with the Christian belief in prioritizing spiritual life over worldly pursuits. While Christians recognized the importance of engaging in their communities and contributing to the common good, their ultimate loyalty was to God, not the state.

This tension between Christian values and Roman expectations were particularly evident in the realm of public service. While some Christians actively participated in Roman politics, many others held back, refusing to compromise their faith by taking oaths of allegiance to the emperor or participating in religious rituals that contradicted their beliefs. This decision often led to accusations of disloyalty and even sedition, further exacerbating tensions between Christians and the Roman authorities.

The Christian emphasis on the sanctity of life and the rejection of violence further amplified the tensions between the Christian faith and the Roman world. While the Roman Empire, like many ancient societies, relied on military power and conquest to maintain its dominance, Christians were taught to follow the teachings of Jesus, who called for love, forgiveness, and non-violent resistance. This pacifist stance, while admirable from a moral perspective, often presented practical challenges in a world where violence was frequently used as a tool of both defense and aggression.

The Roman world also had a strong emphasis on traditional family structures and social roles. The patriarchal system, where men held authority over women and children, was deeply ingrained in Roman society. This societal norm clashed with the Christian emphasis on the equality of all people in the eyes of God and the rejection of arbitrary hierarchies based on gender.

While respecting traditional family structures, Christians sought to redefine the roles of husbands and wives, promoting mutual respect and love within the family unit. They challenged the Roman tradition of male dominance, asserting the equal dignity of women and advocating for their involvement in the church's life.

The early Christians found themselves navigating a complex and often hostile social landscape. While their commitment to faith and love was a source of strength, it also brought them into conflict with the prevailing norms of the Roman world. The challenges they faced required a delicate balance of adherence to their beliefs and accommodation to the demands of their society, a struggle that played a crucial role in shaping the development of Christianity and its enduring legacy.

30. THE TRANSFORMATION OF CHRISTIANITY FROM A PERSECUTED MINORITY TO A DOMINANT FORCE

The transformation of Christianity from a persecuted minority to a dominant force within the Roman Empire was a complex and multifaceted process. It wasn't a sudden shift but a gradual evolution influenced by various factors. The early Christians, initially viewed with suspicion and hostility, eventually became a powerful and influential presence within Roman society.

Several key factors contributed to this remarkable change. The persecution, while brutal, served as a catalyst for the growth of the Christian community. Persecutions, often sporadic and localized, fueled the determination of believers and their sense of solidarity. They also drew attention to faith, making it more visible and attracting converts who were inspired by the resilience and unwavering faith of those who endured hardship. The early Christians, often drawn from the marginalized and lower social classes, found a sense of belonging and purpose in Christianity. They formed tight-knit communities that offered support, shared resources, and provided a refuge from the injustices of the Roman world.

The teachings of Jesus, emphasizing love, forgiveness, and compassion, resonated deeply with many who felt disenfranchised by the Roman system. Christianity's message of equality and salvation regardless of social status appealed to those seeking an alternative to the prevailing social order. As Christianity spread, it encountered diverse cultures, influencing and being influenced by them. Early Christians adapted their practices and expressions of faith, incorporating elements of Roman culture while maintaining their core beliefs. This flexibility helped them gain acceptance among various groups and facilitated the spread of the faith.

The role of prominent early Christian leaders like Paul, Peter, and others was critical in expanding the faith beyond its Jewish origins. Paul's missionary journeys to various parts of the Roman Empire established new Christian communities and churches. Initially facing opposition and even persecution, these communities became centers of learning, charity, and service. The early church's emphasis on love, compassion, and social justice had a tangible impact on Roman society. They established schools, hospitals, and charitable organizations, aiding the poor, sick, and marginalized. These acts of kindness and service demonstrated the practical effects of their faith and earned them the respect and admiration of many Romans.

Moreover, the political landscape of the Roman Empire also played a significant role. The Roman emperors, grappling with internal and external challenges, saw in Christianity a potential stabilizing force. Constantine the Great's conversion to Christianity in the early 4th century CE marked a turning point. He saw Christianity as a unifying force that could promote social cohesion and strengthen the empire. Constantine's support for Christianity was instrumental in its rapid growth and acceptance. He established churches, granted Christians freedom of worship, and ended persecution. His actions paved the way for Christianity's ascension as the dominant religion of the Roman Empire.

The Edict of Milan in 313 CE formally granted tolerance for Christianity throughout the empire. By the end of the 4th century CE, Christianity had become the Roman Empire's official religion. This shift had profound implications for both Christianity and the empire. Christianity, once a persecuted minority, now held significant influence in shaping the Roman world's political, social, and cultural landscape. It impacted laws, education, art, architecture, and the very fabric of Roman society. The Roman Empire, in turn, provided a structure for Christianity to grow and spread. The vast network of roads, communication systems, and legal framework facilitated the organization and administration of the Christian Church.

The transformation of Christianity from a persecuted minority to a dominant force was not without its complexities and challenges. The rise of Christianity also led to internal conflicts and theological debates, shaping the development of Christian doctrine and the emergence of different branches of the faith. As Christianity became intertwined with the Roman state, it faced new challenges. The church's growing influence led to questions about the balance of power between religious and secular authority.

The relationship between Christianity and the Roman Empire evolved over time. The shift from persecution to acceptance, then to dominance, was marked by both cooperation and tension. Despite the complex and sometimes challenging nature of this dynamic, the influence of the Roman Empire on early Christianity is undeniable. It shaped the church's organization, growth, and development, ultimately contributing to its transformation into one of the world's major religions. The early Christians, driven by their faith and commitment to love and compassion, ultimately achieved what seemed unimaginable: a minority faith challenging and transforming one of the mightiest empires in history. Their story serves as a reminder that even the seemingly insignificant can become a powerful force for change when driven by a profound belief and a commitment to their principles.

31. THE SIGNIFICANCE OF THE CHURCH FATHERS

The Church Fathers, a constellation of theologians, writers, and spiritual leaders who emerged in the first few centuries of Christianity, played a pivotal role in shaping the nascent Christian faith. Their writings and teachings, born from a time of intense intellectual and theological ferment, served as the bedrock upon which the Christian tradition was built. They wrestled with fundamental questions about the nature of God, the person of Christ, the meaning of salvation, and the church's role in the world, their answers profoundly influencing subsequent Christian thought and practice.

These early giants of the faith, often referred to as "the Fathers," came from diverse backgrounds and wielded their unique gifts in service to the Christian community. Some, like Augustine of Hippo and John Chrysostom, were renowned preachers, their sermons resonating with audiences across the Roman Empire and beyond. Others, like Clement of Alexandria and Origen, were prolific writers, their treatises and commentaries on scripture becoming foundational texts for theological study and debate. Still others, like Ambrose of Milan and Gregory the Great, were prominent bishops, their leadership shaping the development of church governance and practice.

The Church Fathers' contributions were multifaceted. They provided intellectual rigor to the developing Christian worldview, grappling with philosophical questions about the nature of reality, the existence of evil, and the relationship between reason and faith. Their systematic theological formulations, often born from heated debates with dissenting voices, served to clarify and define essential Christian doctrines. They also laid the groundwork for Christian spirituality, offering insights into prayer, contemplation, and the pursuit of holiness.

Furthermore, their literary legacy is immense. Through their sermons, treatises, and letters, they preserved and transmitted the scriptures and enriched the burgeoning Christian literature. Their writings became models for future generations of Christian authors, their eloquence and depth of thought shaping the language of faith and spirituality.

Their translations of the Bible, particularly Jerome's Latin Vulgate, ensured that the sacred texts were accessible to wider audiences and served as a bridge between the ancient world and subsequent generations.

The Church Fathers were also profoundly involved in the practicalities of church life. They addressed issues like organizing church governance, developing liturgical practices, and establishing charitable institutions. Their influence extended beyond theological circles, permeating the social fabric of the Roman Empire and beyond. They advocated for social justice, offered guidance on ethical conduct, and provided solace and support to those in need.

The Church Fathers' significance lies not only in their individual contributions but also in their collective impact on the course of Christianity. They bridged the gap between the early apostolic church and subsequent generations, shaping the Christian tradition and its understanding of itself. They provided a framework for interpreting scripture, articulating key doctrines, and establishing practices that continue to resonate in churches worldwide.

Their influence extends beyond the realm of theology and spirituality. The Church Fathers' writings, steeped in the cultural and intellectual landscape of the Roman world, offer valuable insights into the history of ideas, the development of language, and the intersection of faith and culture. Their grappling with questions of justice, poverty, and social responsibility remains relevant in the modern world, reminding us of the enduring ethical and social commitments at the heart of the Christian faith.

Exploring the lives and legacies of the Church Fathers is not merely an academic exercise but a journey of profound spiritual and intellectual discovery. Their writings offer a window into the hearts and minds of early Christians, their struggles, triumphs, and unwavering commitment to the message of Jesus. Their legacy invites us to engage with the enduring questions they grappled with, prompting us to reflect on our relationship with faith, tradition, and the ever-evolving landscape of our contemporary world.

Augustine of Hippo

Augustine of Hippo, born in 354 CE in Thagaste, North Africa, stands as a towering figure in the history of Christian thought. His intellectual prowess, personal struggles, and profound theological insights left an indelible mark on the development of the Western church, shaping not only Christian doctrine but also philosophy and Western civilization itself. His life, a fascinating blend of intellectual pursuit, spiritual searching, and profound transformation, offers a compelling narrative for understanding the evolution of early Christianity.

Augustine's early life was marked by intellectual curiosity and a restless search for truth. He immersed himself in the philosophical and rhetorical traditions of his time, becoming a skilled orator and a prominent figure in the Manichean sect, a dualistic religious movement that sought to reconcile the existence of good and evil. However, despite his intellectual accomplishments, Augustine remained dissatisfied, yearning for a deeper understanding of the world and his place in it.

A pivotal turning point in Augustine's life came through the influence of Ambrose, the Bishop of Milan. Witnessing Ambrose's eloquence and witnessing generated the profound impact of his sermons on the lives of others, Augustine began to question the limitations of Manichaeism and to seek a more satisfying spiritual path. The encounter with Ambrose's teachings and the profound experience of conversion that followed are vividly described in Augustine's autobiographical work, Confessions.

In Confessions, Augustine recounts his struggle with sin, his pursuit of knowledge and pleasure, and the transformative power of God's grace. The book considered a masterpiece of Christian literature, offers a deeply personal exploration of the human condition, the nature of faith, and the struggle between human desire and divine will. Augustine's exploration of his inner turmoil and his ultimate surrender to God's love has resonated with countless readers throughout the ages, providing a profound and relatable portrayal of the human journey toward faith.

Augustine's theological contributions were profound and enduring. He championed the Church's orthodox teachings, particularly those related to the nature of God, the Trinity, and the relationship between grace and human freedom. His writings, including City of God, On Christian Doctrine, and On the Trinity, are considered seminal works in Christian theology, shaping the development of Western Christianity for centuries to come.

The City of God, written in response to the sack of Rome by the Visigoths in 410 CE, offers a profound theological and philosophical reflection on the nature of history and the two cities: the City of God, representing the realm of faith and eternal life, and the City of Man, representing the realm of earthly desires and temporal affairs. Augustine's analysis of history as a struggle between these two cities, guided by the tension between divine providence and human free will, provided a powerful framework for understanding the course of human events and the ultimate destiny of humanity.

Augustine's theological innovations extended to his understanding of grace and human freedom. He fiercely defended the concept of divine grace as the ultimate source of salvation, emphasizing God's initiative in redeeming humanity. However, he also acknowledged the importance of human freedom and responsibility, asserting that while God's grace is necessary for salvation, individuals still have the capacity to choose between good and evil. This intricate relationship between grace and freedom became a defining theme in Augustine's theology, and a cornerstone of Western Christian thought.

Augustine's profound impact on the development of Christian doctrine, philosophy, and the Western church are undeniable. His writings have been studied, debated, and interpreted by theologians, philosophers, and scholars for centuries, influencing countless individuals and shaping the intellectual landscape of the West. His exploration of human nature, sin, and redemption, his defense of orthodox Christian teachings and his insights into the relationship between faith and reason continue to resonate with readers today.

Augustine's legacy extends beyond the realm of theology. He is considered a foundational figure in Western philosophy, influencing the development of philosophical ideas about epistemology, metaphysics, and political thought. His ideas about the nature of truth, the role of reason, and the relationship between the individual and society have profoundly impacted the development of Western philosophical thought, shaping the intellectual landscape of the West.

Furthermore, Augustine's emphasis on the importance of internal experience, introspection, and the search for meaning remains relevant in our contemporary world. In an increasingly secular and complex society, Augustine's writings offer insights into the human search for meaning and purpose, the struggle with sin and temptation, and the enduring power of faith in the face of adversity.

In conclusion, Augustine of Hippo stands as a giant of early Christian thought, his life and writings leaving an enduring legacy on the development of Christianity, philosophy, and Western civilization. His intellectual brilliance, personal struggles, and profound theological insights continue to inspire and challenge readers today, offering a compelling testament to the transformative power of faith and the enduring search for truth and meaning.

32. THE INFLUENCE OF JEROME AND HIS TRANSLATION OF THE BIBLE

Jerome, born Eusebius Hieronymus Sophronius in Stridon, a town on the border of Pannonia and Dalmatia (modern-day Croatia), in approximately 347 AD, emerged as a pivotal figure in the history of the Church, particularly for his profound influence on the transmission of the Bible to generations of Christians. He was a man of extraordinary intellect, vast learning, and unwavering commitment to the Christian faith, and both intellectual pursuits and a deep sense of religious fervor marked his life. His passion for scholarship, coupled with a fervent devotion to the Scriptures propelled him to undertake a monumental task—translating the Bible into Latin.

Jerome's early years were steeped in education. He received a comprehensive education in the classical languages, including Greek and Latin, and developed a keen interest in rhetoric, literature, and philosophy. This early exposure to classical learning would later serve him well in his work as a translator and interpreter of Scripture. His intellectual prowess was evident from an early age, as he was known for his sharp wit and insightful observations. However, despite his intellectual brilliance, Jerome harbored a restlessness within him, a longing for something beyond the confines of secular learning. He felt a growing conviction that his true calling lay in the service of the Church and the pursuit of a deeper understanding of the Scriptures.

This spiritual awakening led him to embrace Christianity, which transformed his life. He embarked on a journey of spiritual exploration, seeking guidance from prominent figures in the Church. One of his mentors was the renowned scholar and theologian Donatus, from whom he received instruction in the principles of biblical interpretation. This encounter solidified Jerome's commitment to a life of faith and scholarship, and he became increasingly convinced that translating the Bible into Latin was a crucial task that needed to be undertaken.

His quest for spiritual growth led him to Rome, where he was ordained as a priest in 379 AD. In Rome, he immersed himself in the intellectual and theological milieu of the city, rubbing shoulders with leading thinkers and writers. His sharp intellect and profound knowledge of Scripture quickly made him a sought-after commentator and scholar. He began writing commentaries on biblical texts, engaging in theological debates, and contributing to the Church's intellectual life. He also closely connected with the influential Roman matron Paula and her daughter, Eustochium, who shared his passion for biblical study.

Jerome's time in Rome was a period of intense intellectual and spiritual growth, but it was also marked by internal struggles. He grappled with the tension between his love of classical learning and his devotion to the Scriptures. His deep knowledge of Latin literature and his understanding of rhetoric led him to question the quality of the existing Latin translations of the Bible, which he deemed inadequate and lacking in fidelity to the original Greek and Hebrew texts. This dissatisfaction would eventually lead him to embark on the monumental task of translating the Bible into Latin.

Seeking greater solitude and freedom to pursue his studies, Jerome, accompanied by Paula and Eustochium, left Rome in 382 AD and traveled to the Holy Land. He settled in Bethlehem, a location steeped in biblical significance, where he established a monastery and dedicated himself to the task of translating the Scriptures. He lived a life of austerity and intense study, immersing himself in the Hebrew and Greek texts and meticulously comparing them to existing Latin translations. His meticulous approach to translation was driven by a deep desire to ensure accuracy and fidelity to the original text, and his commitment to the Hebrew language allowed him to produce translations that were more faithful to the original than those that had come before.

Jerome's monumental undertaking was not without its challenges. The existing Latin translations were deeply entrenched in the tradition of the Church, and there was resistance to his efforts to introduce a new version. Some scholars argued that his translations were too literal and lacked the poetic beauty and rhetorical flourishes characteristic of traditional Latin prose. However, Jerome remained unwavering in his belief that the Scriptures should be accessible to all Christians in a faithful and accurate translation.

His translation of the Bible into Latin, known as the Vulgate, became a landmark achievement in the history of the Church. Jerome's work was groundbreaking in its meticulous attention to detail, commitment to the original Hebrew and Greek texts, and clarity and elegance of language.

The Vulgate, meaning "common" or "popular," quickly gained acceptance as the standard translation of the Bible in the Latin-speaking world, effectively replacing the earlier, less accurate translations. It was the foundational text for centuries of theological scholarship, liturgical practices, and Christian literature. It became the Bible of the Western Church, shaping the understanding and interpretation of Scripture for generations of Christians.

The impact of Jerome's work extends far beyond the realm of biblical translation. His deep knowledge of the Scriptures, his eloquence as a writer, and his tireless scholarship made him a highly influential figure in developing Christian theology and literature. He wrote extensively, producing commentaries on biblical texts, polemical works against heresies, letters to friends and colleagues, and devotional writings. His writings were characterized by their intellectual rigor, their spiritual depth, and their vivid and engaging style.

Among his most influential works were his commentaries on the Gospels, which offered insightful interpretations of Jesus' teachings and parables. His commentary on the book of Psalms, known as the "Psalter," became a foundational text for developing Christian psalmody. His works against heresies, such as the "Against the Pelagians," defended the orthodox Christian understanding of grace and predestination. His letters, which offered insights into the intellectual and spiritual life of the Church, are invaluable sources for understanding the history and culture of the early Christian era.

Jerome's legacy is one of scholarship, faith, and unwavering dedication to the Word of God. He stands as a pivotal figure in the history of the Church, not only for his translation of the Bible into Latin but also for his contributions to the development of Christian theology, literature, and scholarship. The Vulgate, his monumental achievement, has served as the primary text for the Western Church for centuries, shaping the understanding and interpretation of Scripture for countless Christians. His writings, characterized by their intellectual rigor, spiritual depth, and vibrant style, continue to be studied and admired by scholars and theologians alike. His commitment to the Scriptures, love of learning, and tireless pursuit of truth have left an enduring mark on the Church and its ongoing quest for a deeper understanding of the Word of God.

Jerome's life and work offer a compelling example of the profound impact that scholarship and faith can have on the world. His dedication to the Scriptures, his intellectual prowess, and his unwavering pursuit of truth have left an enduring legacy that continues to inspire and guide Christians today. He stands as a testament to the power of faith, learning, and the transformative potential of translating the Word of God into the people's language. His work reminds us of the importance of engaging with the Scriptures in a spirit of humility, rigor, and love and of seeking to understand the Word of God with clarity and faithfulness.

33. THE CONTRIBUTIONS OF OTHER PROMINENT CHURCH FATHERS

The contributions of these Church Fathers to the early church were profound and multifaceted. Athanasius, the Bishop of Alexandria, was a staunch defender of the Nicene Creed and a key figure in the fight against Arianism, a heresy that denied the divinity of Christ. His writings, like "On the Incarnation" and "Against the Arians," remain pivotal theological texts. His tireless efforts to uphold the true nature of Christ, despite facing persecution and exile, solidified his place as a pillar of the early church. He is considered one of the most influential figures in the development of Trinitarian doctrine, a cornerstone of Christian faith.

Gregory of Nazianzus, a brilliant orator and theologian, was known for his eloquent sermons and insightful theological works. He is credited with popularizing the term "homoousios," meaning "of the same substance," which became a crucial element in the Nicene Creed. Gregory's writings, including his "Oration 31: On the Theology of the Holy Trinity" and "Oration 40: On the Son," provided profound insights into the nature of the Trinity and the relationship between the Father, Son, and Holy Spirit. His profound theological contributions and persuasive arguments shaped the early church's understanding of God's nature and the Christian faith.

Gregory of Nyssa, the younger brother of Gregory of Nazianzus was a philosopher and theologian who explored various theological themes. He was particularly known for his insightful writings on Christology, soteriology (the study of salvation), and the human soul. His work "On the Soul and the Resurrection" is a masterpiece of early Christian literature offers a detailed exploration of the nature of the human soul and its connection to the divine. He also contributed significantly to developing Christian mysticism, emphasizing the mystical union between humanity and God. Gregory's contributions to theology, philosophy, and spirituality left an enduring mark on the early church and continue to resonate with theologians and philosophers today.

John Chrysostom, "Golden-Mouthed" John, was a renowned preacher and expositor of Scripture. Known for his captivating eloquence and powerful sermons, he delivered impactful homilies on various biblical texts, addressing issues like sin, repentance, and the Christian life. His homilies on the Gospel of Matthew and the Epistles of Paul remain valuable resources for understanding and applying the Scriptures to daily life. He was also a vocal advocate for social justice and the needs of the poor, calling for the wealthy to share their resources with the less fortunate. John Chrysostom's emphasis on practical Christianity and his passion for social justice left a lasting impact on the church and inspired generations of preachers and social reformers.

These are just a few examples of the many notable Church Fathers who shaped the early church. Their lives and legacies offer a glimpse into the early Christian era's intellectual vibrancy and theological richness. Their writings, sermons, and actions serve as a testament to the enduring power of the Christian faith and its influence on the development of Western civilization. By studying their contributions, we gain a deeper understanding of the origins of Christian thought, the diversity of early Christian perspectives, and the enduring relevance of these foundational ideas.

34. CHAPTER THE ENDURING LEGACY OF THE CHURCH FATHERS

The Church Fathers, those giants of early Christian thought and practice, left an indelible mark on the faith that resonates deeply in today's Christian world. Their contributions to theology, liturgy, and the development of Christian tradition have shaped the very fabric of the church, influencing everything from the core beliefs of Christianity to the rituals and practices of worship.

Their influence began with the very foundation of Christian theology. Through their writings, the Church Fathers meticulously articulated the essential tenets of the faith, grappling with profound questions about the nature of God, the person of Christ, and the relationship between the divine and the human. They painstakingly built upon the teachings of the Apostles and the scriptures, drawing on their knowledge of Scripture, philosophy, and the burgeoning intellectual landscape of their time. The resulting theological framework established by the Church Fathers laid the foundation for generations of subsequent theologians and shaped the theological landscape of Christianity for centuries to come.

Their influence extended far beyond theological doctrines, shaping how Christians worship and practice their faith. They played a crucial role in developing the liturgical practices of the early church, contributing to the formation of prayer patterns, sacraments, and the structure of worship services. The Church Fathers brought their wisdom and insight to bear on the development of liturgical elements that would endure for centuries, shaping how Christians engage in prayer, celebrate communion, and practice their faith in community.

Beyond theology and liturgy, the Church Fathers played a pivotal role in shaping the emerging Christian tradition. Their writings provided a rich tapestry of historical accounts, biographical sketches, and philosophical reflections that contributed to developing a uniquely Christian worldview. They meticulously compiled and preserved the writings of early Christians, carefully preserving the scriptural texts, the writings of the Apostles, and other important documents that would form the foundation of the Christian library. In doing so, they ensured that the historical and theological legacy of the early church would be passed down through generations, serving as a source of inspiration and guidance for countless Christians.

One of the most significant legacies of the Church Fathers is their contribution to developing Christian literature. Their writings, encompassing various genres, including theological treatises, letters, sermons, and biographies, became essential texts for the developing Christian community. These writings served as powerful vehicles for communicating the teachings of the faith, shaping the understanding of Scripture, and fostering the growth of Christian thought.

The Church Fathers also played a crucial role in disseminating Christian ideas beyond the boundaries of the early church. Their writings and teachings traveled far and wide, influencing the development of Christian communities in diverse regions and contributing to the expansion of the Christian faith across the Roman Empire and beyond. They acted as bridges between the early church and the broader intellectual landscape, engaging with the philosophical currents of their time and adapting Christian ideas for a wider audience.

The enduring legacy of the Church Fathers is evident in the continued relevance of their writings and teachings. Their insights into human nature, the search for meaning, and the profound mystery of faith continue to resonate with Christians today. Their writings, translated and studied for centuries, remain vital for spiritual guidance and theological reflection.

The impact of the Church Fathers is not limited to the intellectual and spiritual realms. Their legacy is also evident in the cultural and societal contributions of Christianity.

Their teachings on love, compassion, and social justice inspired a rich tradition of charitable works, educational initiatives, and social reform movements that continue to shape today's world.

The Church Fathers' enduring influence lies in their commitment to building a vibrant and enduring Christian community. They were theologians, writers, preachers, and leaders who dedicated their lives to nurturing the faith and shaping the church's future. Their tireless efforts laid the foundation for a tradition that would continue to grow, evolve, and inspire countless Christians for centuries to come.

Their legacy is a powerful reminder of the profound impact that individual lives can have on the course of history and the enduring power of faith. The Church Fathers, those giants of early Christianity, continue to inspire and challenge us to engage in the ongoing conversation about faith, to grapple with the enduring questions that lie at the heart of our humanity, and to strive to live lives of love, service, and faith in the world.

In conclusion, the Church Fathers' enduring legacy is woven into the very fabric of Christianity. Their contributions to theology, liturgy, and the development of Christian tradition have shaped the church, influencing everything from core beliefs to how Christians worship. Their writings remain a vital source of inspiration and guidance for Christians today, reminding us of the power of faith, the enduring value of intellectual inquiry, and the importance of building a vibrant and enduring community. Their legacy continues to inspire generations of Christians to live lives of faith, service, and love in the world.

35. THE ORIGINS AND DEVELOPMENT OF MONASTICISM

The origins of monasticism can be traced back to the early Christian centuries, a time when many sought a deeper connection with God and a more profound experience of faith. This movement was characterized by a withdrawal from the complexities of societal life and a dedication to a life of prayer, contemplation, and service. While it is difficult to pinpoint the exact moment monasticism emerged, its roots can be found in the teachings of Jesus and the early Christian community's emphasis on living a life of self-denial and devotion.

The first wave of monasticism arose in the Egyptian desert during the 3rd and 4th centuries. In this harsh and desolate landscape, individuals like Saint Anthony the Great found solace and a deeper connection with God.

Seeking a life of solitude and contemplation, Anthony abandoned his worldly possessions and retreated into the desert to live a life of extreme austerity, devotion to prayer, and self-discipline. His example inspired others to follow in his footsteps, leading to the formation of small communities of hermits and anchorites living in isolated cells, caves, and tombs. These individuals, seeking to escape the distractions and temptations of the world, devoted themselves to prayer, fasting, and studying Scripture.

However, monasticism did not only manifest as solitary endeavors. Saint Pachomius, another prominent figure in the early monastic movement, established Egypt's first structured monastic communities. In the 4th century, Pachomius organized groups of monks living together under a set of rules that governed their daily life, emphasizing communal prayer, manual labor, and obedience to a superior.

These early communities served as models for later monastic organizations, fostering a spirit of fellowship, discipline, and service.

The appeal of monasticism extended beyond the boundaries of Egypt. It spread throughout the Roman Empire, drawing individuals seeking a more profound spiritual experience and a life dedicated to God. By the 5th century, monasticism had taken root in regions such as Syria, Palestine, and Mesopotamia. The flourishing of monasticism in these regions resulted in the establishment of diverse monastic orders, each adhering to its own set of rules and practices.

The westward expansion of monasticism marked a significant turning point in the history of this movement. The arrival of monasticism in Western Europe brought about a unique blend of Eastern and Western traditions. Saint Benedict of Nursia, a 6th-century figure, played a pivotal role in shaping the character of Western monasticism. Benedict recognized the need for a structured and unified approach to monastic life and established his own set of rules, known as the Rule of Saint Benedict. This rule, emphasizing moderation, balance, and obedience, became the foundation for countless Benedictine monasteries across Europe.

The Rule of Saint Benedict encouraged balanced prayer, contemplation, and work life. Benedictine monks were expected to engage in manual labor, contributing to the self-sufficiency of their communities. They were also required to participate in regular prayer services, study Scripture, and reflect spiritually. The Rule of Saint Benedict fostered a sense of community and encouraged monks to live a life of simplicity, service, and dedication to God.

The spread of monasticism had a profound impact on Western Christianity. Monasteries became centers of learning, preserving knowledge and fostering intellectual pursuits. They also played a significant role in the development of Christian scholarship, translating and copying manuscripts, producing illuminated Bibles, and preserving the writings of the Church Fathers.

Beyond intellectual pursuits, monasteries became centers of social service. They provided shelter for the poor and the sick, offered hospitality to travelers, and engaged in charitable work, embodying the Christian principles of compassion and service. Monasteries played a crucial role in developing healthcare, agriculture, and the arts, leaving a lasting legacy on Western civilization.

The enduring influence of monasticism cannot be overstated. It has left an indelible mark on Christian spirituality, fostering a deep connection with God, a commitment to a life of prayer and contemplation, and a dedication to service. Monasticism has also shaped the development of Christian theology, contributing to the interpretation of Scripture, the articulation of Christian doctrine, and the evolution of spiritual practices.

However, monasticism has not always been without its challenges. Monastic communities have faced internal disputes, doctrinal controversies, and external pressures throughout history. Some monastic orders have struggled with maintaining discipline, addressing accusations of corruption, and adapting to changing social and cultural landscapes. Despite these challenges, monasticism remains a vibrant and influential Christian force, offering a unique and timeless path to spiritual growth and service.

36.   THE EARLY MONASTIC COMMUNITIES AND THEIR IMPACT

The seeds of Christian monasticism were sown in the arid deserts of Egypt in the third century, a time when a growing number of Christians sought a deeper connection with God.

Driven by a yearning for spiritual renewal and a desire to escape the distractions of urban life, these early monastics retreated to remote caves, mountains, and desolate landscapes. Among them emerged figures like Saint Anthony the Great, considered the "Father of Monasticism," inspired by the Gospel's teachings, chose to live in solitude, dedicating himself to prayer, contemplation, and asceticism. He sought to emulate the life of Jesus, embracing poverty, chastity, and obedience as pillars of his existence.

Anthony's example resonated with others, leading to small, isolated communities where individuals committed to a life of prayer and service. These early monastic communities, often called "cenobites," lived together under a shared rule guided by a spiritual leader known as an abbot or abbess. Their days were structured around a regimen of prayer, work, and study, seeking to cultivate virtue and holiness through a disciplined lifestyle.

The early monastics developed a unique set of practices designed to deepen their spiritual lives. These included:

Lectio Divina:
A method of prayerfully reading and reflecting on Scripture, seeking to encounter God's word and its application to their lives.

Asceticism:
A disciplined practice of self-denial, involving fasting, physical labor, and the rejection of material possessions, seeking to subdue the desires of the flesh and cultivate spiritual growth.

Contemplation:
A practice of quiet contemplation and meditation, seeking to enter into a deep communion with God and experience divine presence.

Manual Labor:
Engaging in physical labor, often farming or craftwork, as a means of self-sufficiency and a tangible expression of service to God and others.

While the early monastics initially sought solitude, the need for guidance and support led to the formation of communities. These communities became centers of learning, where monks and nuns transcribed ancient texts, preserved knowledge, and developed theological insights. They played a vital role in shaping early Christian spirituality, emphasizing the importance of prayer, contemplation, and service while fostering a culture of scholarship and intellectual exploration.

The early monastics were not merely isolated individuals pursuing personal piety. They served the broader community, providing food, shelter, and medical care to the poor and sick. Their monasteries became refuges for those seeking spiritual direction, education, and refuge from the trials of the world. Through their lives of prayer and service, they embodied the values of the Gospel, exemplifying humility, compassion, and unwavering devotion to God.

The influence of these early monastic communities extended far beyond their immediate surroundings. The monastic way of life spread rapidly, reaching beyond the deserts of Egypt and into other regions of the Roman

Empire. Monasticism became a vital force in shaping the development of Christian spirituality, theology, and culture.

Notable figures who shaped the development of early monasticism include:

Saint Pachomius:
He established the first structured

monastic community in Egypt in the 4th century, introducing a communal life based on a shared rule and emphasizing obedience, labor, and communal prayer.

Saint Basil the Great:
In the 4th century, he formulated a rule for monastic communities in the Eastern Church, emphasizing spiritual growth, communal living, and a balanced life of prayer, work, and service.

Saint Jerome:
A renowned scholar and translator, Jerome lived as a hermit in the 4th and 5th centuries, contributing significantly to the development of monastic life in the West. His translation of the Bible into Latin, known as the Vulgate, became the standard text for the Catholic Church for centuries.

The early monastic communities also contributed significantly to the development of Christian theology. Monks and nuns dedicated themselves to studying Scripture, engaging in theological debates, and writing commentaries on the Bible and other theological texts. They were instrumental in preserving and transmitting knowledge, contributing to Christian thought and scholarship development. Their contributions shaped the theological landscape of the early church, leaving an enduring legacy on Christian doctrine and spirituality.

The spread of monasticism to the West marked a turning point in the development of Christian life. Saint Benedict of Nursia, a 6th-century Italian monk, established a monastic rule that profoundly shaped Western monasticism. His rule, known as the Rule of Saint Benedict, emphasized a balanced life of prayer, work, and service, fostering a strong sense of community and obedience to God. Benedictine monasteries became centers of learning, agriculture, and charitable work, playing a vital role in preserving knowledge, providing education, and contributing to their communities' social and economic well-being.

Monasticism's impact on Christianity and society has been profound. It fostered a culture of contemplation, scholarship, and service, shaping Christian spirituality and influencing the development of Western civilization. Monasteries became centers of learning, preserving ancient texts, and transmitting knowledge across generations. They played a pivotal role in the development of art, literature, and architecture, contributing to Europe's cultural and intellectual landscape.

37. THE LEGACY OF EARLY MONASTICISM CONTINUES TO RESONATE TODAY.

Many monastic orders, rooted in the early traditions, still thrive, offering a way of life dedicated to prayer, contemplation, and service. Their contributions to Christian spirituality, scholarship, and society have left an enduring mark on the world, reminding us of the power of seeking a deeper connection with God, embracing a life of service, and seeking to live in accordance with the teachings of the Gospel.

The Influence of Saint Anthony and Saint Pachomius

The lives of Saint Anthony the Great and Saint Pachomius stand as testaments to the transformative power of early Christian spirituality. They emerged as influential figures during a period of burgeoning monasticism, leaving an indelible mark on the development of this unique form of religious life. Their stories resonate with profound implications for understanding the spiritual landscape of the 4th century and the enduring impact of their choices on Christian history.

Saint Anthony, born around 251 AD in Egypt, is a pivotal figure in the origins of monasticism. He was a young man of privilege, yet he renounced worldly possessions and embraced a life of solitude in the Egyptian desert. Inspired by the teachings of Jesus and the biblical stories of hermits like Elijah, Anthony sought a more intense and focused relationship with God, a pursuit that led him to a life of rigorous asceticism. He spent years living in a cave, subsisting on minimal food and water, enduring extreme temperatures, and dedicating himself to prayer and contemplation.

Anthony's austere lifestyle attracted others who sought a similar path of spiritual discipline. Disciples flocked to him, seeking his guidance and wisdom, and gradually, a monastic community arose around him. This community, guided by Anthony's principles, established a pattern of life that emphasized self-denial, communal living, and the pursuit of spiritual perfection through labor, prayer, and service. The rules and practices he established became the foundation for a flourishing monastic tradition in Egypt and beyond, influencing the development of cenobitic monasticism, where monks lived together in a community under the guidance of an abbot.

Saint Pachomius, born around 292 AD in Egypt, played a crucial role in shaping monastic communities' organizational structure and practices. He recognized the need for a more structured and coordinated approach to monastic life, which led him to establish a rule for communal living that emphasized obedience, discipline, and a structured schedule of work, prayer, and study. He created the first cenobitic monastery, a communal dwelling for monks, in Tabennesi, Egypt.

Pachomius's monastic rule provided a framework for communal living emphasizes the importance of cooperation and order within the monastic community. He established a leadership hierarchy, with an abbot overseeing the monks and ensuring adherence to the rule. He also introduced a labor system, with each monk assigned specific duties, contributing to the sustenance of the community and fostering a sense of shared responsibility.

The influence of Pachomius extended beyond his own community. Other monastic communities throughout Egypt widely adopted his monastic rule, and his organizational model became a blueprint for the structure and functioning of monastic communities throughout the centuries.

The contributions of Saint Anthony and Saint Pachomius mark a significant turning point in the development of Christian spirituality. They articulated a vision of monastic life that emphasized self-denial, communal living, and the pursuit of spiritual perfection through a disciplined way of life. Their innovations in monastic organization, particularly the emergence of cenobitic monasticism and the establishment of monastic rules, provided a framework for monastic life that endured for centuries.

The impact of their lives and teachings extended far beyond the confines of their monastic communities. They inspired a flourishing monastic movement in Egypt and beyond, influencing the development of monasticism in the East and West. Their emphasis on solitude, contemplation, and service became integral to Christian spirituality, shaping the contemplative practices of individuals and communities throughout the centuries.

Monasticism, as a product of the early church, offered an alternative way of life for Christians who sought a deeper commitment to their faith. This movement found its roots in the desire to emulate the teachings of Jesus and the early disciples, seeking a life of simplicity, service, and spiritual growth. The pursuit of a life of prayer, contemplation, and work, often in isolation from the complexities of society, became a defining characteristic of monasticism.

The contributions of Saint Anthony and Saint Pachomius, along with the numerous monastic communities that followed in their footsteps, significantly impacted the development of Christian spirituality. They established patterns of monastic life that emphasized self-denial, communal living, and the pursuit of spiritual perfection through labor, prayer, and service. This movement not only provided a spiritual path for individuals seeking a deeper connection with God but also fostered the development of theological scholarship, charitable works, and the preservation of knowledge.

The enduring legacy of monasticism lies in its impact on Christian spirituality and its influence on the broader social and cultural landscape. Monastic communities became centers of learning, providing education and preserving knowledge through the copying and disseminating manuscripts.

They also engaged in charitable works, serving the needs of the poor and sick within their communities and beyond.

The influence of monasticism extended to the development of Western civilization. The Benedictine rule, established by Saint Benedict in the 6th century, became a foundational framework for monastic life in the West, shaping the development of Benedictine monastic orders and influencing the evolution of Western culture.

The impact of monasticism is evident in the architecture of monasteries, the art and music produced by monastic communities, and the influence of monastic ideals on the formation of universities and hospitals. The pursuit of a life of contemplation, scholarship, and service, as exemplified by monastic communities, has left a legacy on Christian spirituality and the broader fabric of Western civilization.

38. THE SPREAD OF MONASTICISM TO THE WEST
AND THE ROLE OF SAINT BENEDICT

The seeds of monasticism, planted in the arid sands of the Egyptian desert, began to sprout in the fertile soil of the West. As the Roman Empire embraced Christianity, the monastic ideal, fueled by the desire for spiritual solitude and communion with God, found fertile ground in the West. This westward migration of monasticism was largely driven by the influence of Saint Benedict of Nursia, a figure whose legacy reshaped Western Christianity.

Born in the early 6th century, Benedict sought a life dedicated to God, seeking a sanctuary away from the bustling and often morally corrupt cities of the Roman world. His search for a spiritual haven led him to the hills of central Italy, where he established a monastery at Monte Cassino. Here, Benedict crafted a framework for monastic life, a set of guidelines known as the "Rule of Saint Benedict" that would transform the landscape of Western monasticism.

The Rule of Saint Benedict was a masterpiece of balance, a harmonious blend of spiritual discipline and human compassion. Benedict's emphasis on "Ora et Labora," "Pray and Work," laid the foundation for a life structured around prayer, contemplation, and manual labor. The Rule dictated the rhythm of the monastic day, from the morning prayers and liturgical services to the hours dedicated to manual labor and scripture reading. Benedict understood that work, far from being a mere necessity, could be a form of prayer, a way of offering oneself in service to God and one's community.

The Rule of Saint Benedict emphasized community, fostering a sense of shared purpose and mutual support. The monastery, Benedict envisioned, was not a place of isolated asceticism but a community of brothers bound together by their shared commitment to God. Benedict stressed the importance of humility, obedience, and charity, fostering an environment of mutual respect and care. His Rule outlined guidelines for everything from the structure of meals and the handling of property to the management of disputes and the duties of the abbot, the head of the monastery.

The Rule of Saint Benedict was not meant to be a rigid set of laws but a flexible framework adaptable to the specific needs of each community. Benedict encouraged his monks to live in accordance with the Rule, adapting it as needed to the local context and circumstances. This flexibility proved to be one of the enduring strengths of Benedict's Rule, allowing it to take root in diverse regions and flourish in various environments.

The Rule of Saint Benedict resonated with the spirit of the time, offering a beacon of hope in a world grappling with the decline of the Roman Empire and the turmoil of the early Middle Ages. The Benedictine model of monastic life offered a framework for spiritual renewal and social stability, providing a sense of order and purpose amidst the chaos of the times. Benedictine monasteries became centers of learning, preservation of knowledge, and acts of charity, pivotal in transmitting culture and education throughout the early Middle Ages.

The spread of Benedictine monasticism was a testament to the Rule's power and adaptability. From Monte Cassino, Benedictine monasteries sprung up throughout Europe, each taking on its own unique character while upholding the core principles of the Rule. These monasteries were founded by dedicated monks who sought to live according to Benedict's vision and played a vital role in shaping Europe's cultural and religious landscape. They served as learning centers, preserving the ancient texts of classical literature and Scripture, providing education for future generations, and contributing to developing intellectual and theological discourse.

The impact of Benedictine monasticism extended beyond the walls of monasteries, influencing the lives of ordinary people throughout the Western world. The Benedictine emphasis on work and service inspired the development of agricultural communities, hospitals, and schools, institutions that played a vital role in shaping the social fabric of Europe. Benedictine monks, driven by their commitment to charity, extended their outreach to the wider community, providing aid to the sick and poor, offering hospitality to travelers, and contributing to the welfare of their surrounding regions.

Saint Benedict's legacy and Rule remains deeply ingrained in Western Christianity. Benedictine monasticism, a model of spiritual life that emphasized community, discipline, and service, shaped the development of Western Christianity, fostering a profound sense of faith and devotion. Benedictine orders, established throughout the centuries, continue to uphold the principles of the Rule, contributing to the spiritual and intellectual life of the Church and serving as beacons of faith and hope in the world.

The legacy of Saint Benedict is a testament to the power of a simple Rule that emphasized the fundamental values of prayer, work, and community. His vision resonated deeply with the spirit of the times, offering a framework for spiritual renewal and social stability in a world undergoing profound change. The Benedictine tradition, flourishing for centuries, continues to shape the landscape of Western Christianity,reminding us of the enduring power of a life dedicated to God, service, and the pursuit of spiritual growth.

39. THE LASTING IMPACT OF MONASTICISM ON CHRISTIANITY AND SOCIETY

The rise of monasticism left an indelible mark on Christianity and society extend far beyond the confines of cloistered walls. This movement, born from a desire for a deeper connection with God and a life devoted to spiritual growth, transformed Christian spirituality and shaped culture, education, and the preservation of knowledge. Monasticism's profound impact can be observed in its contributions to theological scholarship, its dedication to charitable works, and its role as a vital repository of ancient wisdom.

Monastic life provided a space for rigorous theological study and reflection. Monks and nuns, freed from the demands of secular life, dedicated themselves to the exploration of scripture and the formulation of Christian doctrine. This intellectual pursuit led to the development of libraries, scriptoria, and schools within monasteries, fostering the growth of theological scholarship and the dissemination of knowledge. The writings of early Church Fathers, many of whom were themselves monks, shaped the foundations of Christian thought, influencing countless generations of theologians and believers. Through their dedication to study and writing, monks played a pivotal role in preserving the legacy of the early church and ensuring its continued relevance.

Beyond intellectual pursuits, monastic communities were known for their commitment to service and charity. The monastic ideal emphasized a life of compassion and a dedication to helping those in need. Monasteries became centers for hospitality, providing shelter and sustenance for travelers, the poor, and the sick. They established hospitals, orphanages, and schools, demonstrating the practical expression of Christian love and compassion.

Through their tireless efforts, monasteries alleviated suffering, promoted social justice, and fostered a culture of service within society.

Monasticism also played a crucial role in preserving and transmitting knowledge during turbulent times. The libraries and scriptoria within monasteries became repositories of ancient texts, safeguarding them from destruction and loss.

Monks meticulously copied manuscripts, ensuring the survival of works of literature, history, philosophy, and scripture. Their dedication to preserving knowledge ensured that the wisdom of the past could be passed on to future generations. Through their tireless efforts in copying, translating, and studying ancient texts, monks became guardians of knowledge, preserving a rich cultural heritage for posterity.

The impact of monasticism extended beyond the confines of monasteries, influencing the broader cultural and social landscape. Monastic communities established schools, fostering education and literacy, which in turn contributed to the advancement of society. Their influence extended to the arts, inspiring architecture, music, and literature. The unique blend of spirituality, scholarship, and service that characterized monastic life became a model for Christian living, influencing religious communities and secular society alike.

In conclusion, the enduring influence of monasticism on Christianity and society is undeniable. From its contributions to theological scholarship and charitable works to its role in preserving knowledge and shaping culture, monasticism left an enduring legacy. Its impact on Christian spirituality, education, and societal values continues to resonate in our world, reminding us of the transformative power of a life dedicated to faith, service, and the pursuit of knowledge.

40. THE SPREAD OF CHRISTIANITY BEYOND THE ROMAN EMPIRE

The spread of Christianity beyond the Roman Empire is a testament to its early appeal and adaptability. While the Roman Empire served as a crucial cradle for the nascent faith, Christianity soon transcended its borders, taking root in diverse regions and cultures and shaping unique expressions of the faith.

The Church in Persia

The early church in Persia, a land steeped in Zoroastrian tradition, emerged through the efforts of merchants and missionaries who traveled along the Silk Road, bringing the Gospel to the heart of the Sassanid Empire. Early Persian Christians, known as "Christians of the East," were drawn to the message of salvation and the concept of a single God, resonating with some Zoroastrian belief aspects.

Their story is intertwined with the challenges of integrating their faith with the prevailing culture and the complexities of navigating a society under Zoroastrian rule. The Christians of Persia faced persecution, most notably during the reign of the Sassanid king Shapur II (309-379 CE), who sought to unify the empire under Zoroastrianism. This persecution, often fueled by a belief that Christianity undermined the stability of the empire, led to the development of underground communities, clandestine gatherings, and a resilience that solidified their commitment to their faith.

Despite the hardships, Christianity thrived, establishing a network of churches, monastic communities, and theological centers. The Persian Church, with its unique blend of biblical tradition and Eastern cultural influences, nurtured a distinctive theological understanding, developing its own liturgical practices and devotional styles. Notable figures like Bardaisan, a 2nd-century Syrian philosopher who integrated elements of Greek philosophy into his Christian teachings, and Marcion, a 2nd-century Gnostic who challenged orthodox Christian beliefs, arose from the Persian Church, sparking theological debates that shaped the development of Christian thought.

The Church in Ethiopia

The spread of Christianity in Ethiopia is often attributed to the legendary figure of Frumentius, a young man who, along with his brother, was shipwrecked off the coast of Ethiopia in the 4th century CE. Impressed by the local people's openness to foreign beliefs, Frumentius became a trusted advisor to the Ethiopian king. He introduced them to the Christian faith, paving the way for the conversion of the ruling elite.

The Ethiopian Church, with its deep roots in ancient traditions, developed unique characteristics, incorporating elements of local culture and beliefs into its Christian practices. They adopted a distinctive version of Christianity, incorporating elements of Jewish tradition and emphasizing the role of the Virgin Mary. The Ethiopian Church also developed its unique liturgical language, Ge'ez, further solidifying its distinctiveness.

The Church in India

The history of Christianity in India is shrouded in layers of speculation and historical debate, but it is widely believed that the apostle Thomas, one of the twelve apostles, traveled to India in the 1st century CE, laying the foundation for the early Christian communities there.

While the exact timeline and extent of Thomas's missionary work remain unclear, archaeological evidence, ancient Christian writings, and the oral traditions of local communities suggest the presence of Christian communities in India as early as the first century CE. These early Christians, often known as "Thomas Christians," embraced the teachings of Jesus, adapting them to the cultural context of India and incorporating elements of local traditions and beliefs into their worship and practice.

Throughout centuries, Christianity in India faced periods of persecution, integration, and growth. The influence of Christianity on the Indian cultural landscape is evident in the architecture of churches, the development of Christian theology in India, and the strong presence of Christian communities in various regions.

41. THE IMPACT OF EARLY CHRISTIANITY BEYOND THE ROMAN EMPIRE

In its spread beyond the Roman Empire, the early church demonstrated its ability to adapt to diverse cultural contexts. Christianity, with its emphasis on a universal message of salvation and its open embrace of different backgrounds, appealed to various individuals and communities, creating a tapestry of diverse expressions of faith.

These early churches, flourishing in Persia, Ethiopia, and India, contributed significantly to the richness and diversity of Christian thought. Each region developed its own unique interpretations of Christian beliefs and practices, incorporating local cultural influences, shaping distinctive liturgical traditions, and contributing to the evolving the landscape of Christian theology.

Despite facing persecution and challenges, these early communities demonstrated the Gospel message's enduring power and its ability to transcend boundaries and transform lives. Their stories, often intertwined with the rich tapestry of history and culture, offer a captivating glimpse into the early Christian world, a world where the faith spread beyond the Roman Empire, taking root in diverse regions and giving rise to vibrant and distinct expressions of the Christian faith.

42. THE IMPACT OF CHRISTIANITY IN DIVERSE
CULTURES

The influence of Christianity spread like wildfire across diverse cultures, transforming ancient civilizations and leaving an indelible mark on the world. It wasn't a one-size-fits-all phenomenon; rather, Christianity adapted to local customs, traditions, and languages, creating a tapestry of faith that reflected the vibrant diversity of the world. This interaction, in turn, shaped the very nature of Christianity itself, creating rich and vibrant expressions of faith that echoed the complexities of human experience.

The early Christians, often ostracized and persecuted, found common ground with individuals from various social strata and cultural backgrounds. They found resonance in their struggles, shared their hopes, and embraced triumphs. This universality of their message resonated with individuals across social, economic, and cultural divides. From the bustling marketplaces of Alexandria to the serene monasteries nestled in the Egyptian desert, Christian communities flourished, bringing light and hope to those who sought meaning and solace.

The early Christians, adept at finding common ground, strategically intertwined Christian teachings with local traditions, which proved both fruitful and strategic. They found ways to bridge cultural divides and build bridges of understanding, showcasing their adaptability and foresight.

In the bustling city of Alexandria, the early Christians interacted with the flourishing Hellenic culture, engaging with the intellectual currents of the time, grappling with the ideas of Greek philosophers, and finding ways to reconcile their faith with the wisdom of the ancient world. This engagement, though challenging, resulted in a rich theological discourse that saw the rise of renowned thinkers like Clement of Alexandria and Origen, who bridged the gap between faith and reason, weaving together Christian teachings with the philosophical insights of ancient Greece.

In the heart of the Roman Empire, Christianity began to take root amidst the grandeur and complexity of Roman society. Early Christians embraced the Roman legal framework, leveraging its institutions to navigate their lives and communities. Though designed to serve a polytheistic culture, the Roman legal system offered a framework that Christianity could adapt. This led to a sophisticated legal framework for Christian communities, allowing them to manage their internal affairs, establish churches, and navigate their relationship with Roman authorities.

The influence of Christianity extended beyond the Mediterranean world, reaching distant lands and diverse cultures. In the vast expanse of North Africa, where the early Christians established thriving communities, the influence of Christianity intertwined with the rich tapestry of African culture. In Ethiopia, a distinctive Christian tradition emerged, drawing from local traditions and the ancient Ethiopian language, creating a unique and vibrant expression of faith.

The early Christians in the region embraced the local language, Ge'ez, preserving ancient texts and translating the Bible into a language accessible to the people. The result was a uniquely Ethiopian Christianity, deeply interwoven with the region's cultural heritage.

As Christianity journeyed east, it encountered the ancient wisdom of the Orient, engaging with philosophies and religions that had shaped civilizations for centuries. In India, Christian communities emerged, embracing local customs and traditions while adapting to the local culture.

This adaptation was a testament to the adaptability and resilience of Christianity, demonstrating its ability to find common ground and resonate with diverse cultures. In China, the early Christians encountered the ancient traditions of Confucianism and Buddhism, sparking rich dialogues that sought to harmonize Christianity with the prevailing philosophical and religious currents of the time.

The tapestry of early Christian history is a testament to the power of adaptation and dialogue. Through their encounters with diverse cultures, the early Christians found ways to bridge cultural divides, creating vibrant expressions of faith that embraced the richness and diversity of the human experience. Their legacy, woven through the fabric of diverse societies, continues to inspire and challenge, reminding us of the transformative power of faith and the enduring message of love and hope that transcends cultural boundaries.

43. THE RISE OF CHRISTIANITY IN THE EAST

The eastward expansion of Christianity took root in the heart of the Roman Empire, where the city of Constantinople, founded by Emperor Constantine in 330 CE, became a new center of power and influence. Situated strategically at the crossroads of East and West, Constantinople became a fertile ground for the growth of Christianity, attracting believers from diverse backgrounds and cultures. The influence of the Greek language and philosophical thought, already evident in the early development of Christian theology, became even more pronounced in the East, shaping the intellectual and religious landscape of the region.

As Christianity flourished in the East, it gradually developed its own distinct theological and liturgical traditions, setting it apart from its Western counterpart. The Eastern Orthodox Church, which emerged as the dominant branch of Christianity in the East, embraced a unique understanding of God, Christ, and the relationship between the divine and the human. The Eastern Orthodox Church emphasized the importance of tradition, icons, and the role of the patriarchs, bishops, and other church leaders in guiding the faithful. It also developed a rich liturgical tradition characterized by elaborate ceremonies, ornate music, and a deep reverence for the sacred.

The Eastern Orthodox Church's emphasis on the divine nature of Christ, its acceptance of the veneration of icons, and strong hierarchical structure set it apart from the Western church, which gradually embraced a more Latin-influenced approach to theology and liturgy. While the Eastern Orthodox Church recognized the authority of the papacy, it maintained a strong sense of independence and autonomy, leading to a growing divide between East and West that would eventually culminate in the Great Schism of 1054 CE.

Despite the theological and liturgical differences between the Eastern and Western churches, Christianity flourished in the East, spreading to diverse regions and cultures. The influence of Eastern Orthodox Christianity extended beyond the borders of the Roman Empire, reaching into areas like Armenia, Georgia, Russia, and the Balkan peninsula. The Eastern Orthodox Church significantly shaped these regions' cultural and social landscape, influencing their art, music, literature, and worldview.

The Eastern Orthodox Church's commitment to the veneration of icons, which it viewed as a window into the divine, gave rise to a rich tradition of iconography that adorned churches and monasteries throughout the East. These icons, painted with meticulous detail and infused with deep spiritual significance, became central to the Orthodox faith, serving as a powerful means of expressing devotion and fostering contemplation.

The Eastern Orthodox Church's emphasis on communal worship and the importance of the liturgy also contributed to the development of a unique form of church architecture characterized by grand cathedrals with soaring domes, intricate mosaics, and opulent interiors. These majestic structures served as a testament to the faith and devotion of the Orthodox faithful, creating a sense of awe and reverence for the divine.

The influence of Eastern Orthodox Christianity extended beyond religious practices and beliefs, shaping the social and cultural life of the regions it embraced. It played a vital role in education, charity, and social reform, establishing monasteries and schools that provided learning and intellectual development opportunities. Eastern Orthodox monasteries, known for their rigorous spiritual discipline and contributions to scholarship, played a crucial role in preserving knowledge and promoting intellectual pursuits, contributing to the development of Eastern culture and civilization.

The growth of Christianity in the East was challenging. The Eastern Orthodox Church faced conflicts with other religions, including Islam, which emerged in the 7th century CE and quickly spread across the Middle East and North Africa. These conflicts often led to periods of persecution and suppression, forcing the Eastern Orthodox Church to adapt and find ways to preserve its faith and traditions in the face of adversity.

Despite the challenges it faced, Eastern Orthodox Christianity continued to flourish in the East, playing a vital role in shaping the cultural and spiritual landscape of the region. It left an indelible mark on the arts, architecture, literature, and philosophy of Eastern cultures, contributing to the rich and diverse tapestry of human civilization. The Eastern Orthodox Church's influence extended beyond the boundaries of religion, impacting the political, social, and cultural life of societies across the East, demonstrating its enduring power and lasting impact on the world.

The legacy of Eastern Orthodox Christianity continues to shape the world today, with millions of believers adhering to its traditions and values. Its rich theological heritage, unique liturgical practices, and emphasis on spiritual growth and communal living have left an enduring imprint on the human experience, reminding us of the enduring power of faith and the transformative impact of belief.

As we move forward in time, we can see how the influence Eastern Orthodox Christianity continued to spread, taking root in new territories and cultures. The church's missionary efforts, driven by a deep commitment to spreading the Gospel message, established Eastern Orthodox churches in various regions of Europe, Asia, and Africa.

For instance, the arrival of Eastern Orthodox Christianity in Russia marked a pivotal moment in its history, profoundly shaping its culture and identity. The church's influence permeated every aspect of Russian life, from art and literature to social customs and political structures. The establishment of the Russian Orthodox Church, which emerged as a powerful institution, solidified the church's presence in the region, becoming a central pillar of Russian identity.

The Eastern Orthodox Church's presence in the Balkans, a region characterized by a blend of cultures and religious traditions, also profoundly impacted. The church's influence in the region helped preserve the Balkan people's cultural heritage, contributing to their unique sense of identity and enduring ties to the Eastern Orthodox faith.

However, the Eastern Orthodox Church's expansion also encountered resistance and conflict, particularly in regions where other religions held sway. The church faced persecution under various regimes, including the Ottoman Empire, which sought to suppress the spread of Christianity in its territories. Despite these challenges, the Eastern Orthodox Church's resilience and unwavering faith allowed it to endure, adapting to changing circumstances and finding ways to preserve its traditions.

As the Eastern Orthodox Church continued to grow and evolve, it also faced internal challenges, including theological disputes and disagreements over matters of doctrine and governance. These debates often resulted in schisms and divisions, leading to the emergence of various branches within the Eastern Orthodox Communion. Despite these internal divisions, the Eastern Orthodox Church's core beliefs and practices remained broadly consistent, united by a shared commitment to the teachings of the early church fathers and the principles of Orthodox Christianity.

The Eastern Orthodox Church's enduring legacy extends beyond its impact on specific regions and cultures. It represents a vibrant and multifaceted branch of Christianity that offers a unique perspective on faith, spirituality, and the human condition. Its rich theological heritage, distinctive liturgical traditions, and emphasis on community and social justice have resonated with believers across the globe, inspiring them to seek a deeper understanding of the Christian faith and live lives of purpose and meaning.

The story of Eastern Orthodox Christianity is a tale of resilience, adaptation, and enduring faith. It reflects the church's ability to navigate complex historical and cultural landscapes while remaining true to its core principles and values. As we continue to study the history of Christianity, we can learn from the Eastern Orthodox Church's example, recognizing the importance of preserving tradition, embracing diversity, and seeking unity amid difference. Its journey offers a compelling testament to the enduring power of faith and the transformative impact of belief on human experience.

44. THE EARLY CHURCHES IN NORTH AFRICA AND THE WEST

The story of Christianity in North Africa and the West is a tapestry woven with threads of vibrant faith, cultural adaptation, and enduring traditions. Unlike its counterparts in the East, Christianity in these regions embraced a more direct relationship with Roman culture, leading to a distinct identity and path of development. The burgeoning Latin Church, nurtured by the fertile soil of Roman influence, emerged as a powerful force, shaping the religious landscape and the very fabric of Western society.

The seeds of Christianity were sown in North Africa during the first century, carried by merchants and missionaries who traversed the bustling trade routes. Early Christian communities flourished in cities like Carthage, Alexandria, and Hippo Regius, drawing converts from diverse social strata, including influential Romans and ordinary citizens. These communities, infused with the fervor of new faith, faced challenges and opportunities. They navigated the complexities of Roman governance, adapted to the local culture, and grappled with the rise of heresies while strengthening their faith and building a lasting legacy.

The Latin Church, a unique expression of Christianity in the West, emerged from this fertile ground. It drew inspiration from the Roman world, adopting its legal structures, administrative systems, and architectural styles. The influence of Latin, the language of the Roman Empire, resonated throughout the Church's development, shaping its liturgy, theological discourse, and written traditions. The Latin Vulgate, a translation of the Bible into Latin by Saint Jerome, became a cornerstone of Western Christianity, solidifying its linguistic and cultural identity.

This adoption of Roman culture had its complexities. While it allowed for a smooth integration of Christianity into the established social order, it also led to tensions between Christian values and Roman practices. The early Church faced persecution under various Roman emperors, with its members enduring imprisonment, torture, and martyrdom for their unwavering faith. Yet, these trials served as a crucible, refining the Church's resolve and forging its resilience.

As Christianity spread throughout North Africa and the West, it encountered diverse cultures and beliefs. In North Africa, the Church engaged in a lively dialogue with ancient pagan traditions, seeking to convert pagans while finding common ground. In the West, the Church encountered the Germanic tribes migrating into the Roman Empire. This encounter led to a fascinating blend of cultures, with the Church adapting its message to resonate with the Germanic worldview while also seeking to shape its beliefs and practices.

The emergence of distinct Western traditions within Christianity is a testament to the Church's ability to adapt and evolve. The theological debates and controversies that shaped the early Church, such as the Arian controversy and the Donatist schism, provided fertile ground for developing distinctive theological interpretations and expressions of faith. The rise of monasticism, particularly the Benedictine order, profoundly influenced Western Christianity, shaping its spirituality, intellectual life, and social organization.

The legacy of early Christianity in North Africa and the West is evident in the enduring institutions, traditions, and cultural expressions that shape the region today. The influence of the Latin Church can be seen in the architecture of cathedrals, the art of the Middle Ages, and the very fabric of Western civilization. The legacy of the early saints, theologians, and reformers continues to inspire generations of believers and scholars.

As we trace the development of Christianity in North Africa and the West, we witness the profound impact of cultural exchange, theological innovation, and enduring faith. The story of these early churches is a testament to Christianity's dynamic nature and its ability to adapt to diverse contexts while preserving its core message. It reminds us that the story of Christianity is not merely a historical record but an ongoing narrative of faith, hope, and transformation, shaping countless individuals' lives and the course of human history.

The Interconnectedness of Early Christian Communities The early Christian communities, though geographically dispersed, were deeply interconnected. This interconnectedness transcended physical boundaries, manifesting in a vibrant exchange of ideas, practices, and influences. These communities' shared experiences, challenges, and triumphs profoundly shaped the nascent Christian faith and contributed to its remarkable growth.

One crucial aspect of this interconnectedness was the exchange of knowledge and theological perspectives. Early Christian thinkers and leaders, driven by a shared passion for understanding their faith, engaged in lively debates and discussions. These discussions, often spurred by challenges from outside the church or internal disputes within the community, resulted in the development of theological frameworks that would define Christian thought for centuries to come. The writings of early Church Fathers like Augustine of Hippo, Jerome, and Athanasius were widely circulated, their ideas forming the foundation for later theological developments. These writings were not confined to a single region but traveled across vast distances, inspiring and challenging Christians in diverse cultures.

The exchange of knowledge extended beyond theological discussions. Early Christian communities shared practices, liturgical traditions, and methods of evangelization. As the faith spread, communities adapted their practices to local contexts, resulting in a rich tapestry of diverse Christian expressions. For example, the development of liturgy in the Eastern Church differed significantly from the West, reflecting the influence of local traditions and the interaction with other cultures. This adaptation did not, however, negate the shared core of the faith, and the communities remained interconnected through their common belief in Jesus Christ, the Bible, and the fundamental tenets of their faith.

The shared experiences of early Christian communities were another crucial factor in their interconnectedness. Persecution, a constant threat in the early centuries of Christianity, fostered a sense of solidarity among believers. Christians in different regions, facing similar challenges, found strength and encouragement in their shared faith. Their experiences of persecution, often documented in the writings of early church leaders, served as a reminder of the cost of discipleship and instilled a commitment to the faith that transcended geographical boundaries.

The spread of Christianity also fostered a shared sense of purpose and mission. The early Christians, united by their belief in the Gospel message, saw themselves as agents of transformation, tasked with sharing their faith with the world. This shared mission, deeply rooted in the teachings of Jesus and the example of the Apostles, propelled them to venture beyond their familiar communities, establishing churches in new regions and cultures.

Furthermore, the interconnectedness of early Christian communities was facilitated by travel and communication. The Roman Empire, with its vast network of roads and its sophisticated system of communication, played a significant role in this process. Early Christians, driven by the desire to share their faith or seek guidance from other communities, traveled extensively, spreading the Gospel and fostering dialogue. Letters exchanged between different communities, particularly the letters of the Apostles and other early church leaders, provided a vital channel for disseminating information, conveying theological perspectives, and fostering unity among believers.

This interconnectedness, though often invisible in historical accounts, was a vital force shaping growth and development of early Christianity. It enabled the exchange of knowledge, the sharing of practices, and the creation of a shared sense of purpose and mission among believers. Despite their diversity and geographical separation, The early Christian communities were deeply connected, united by a shared faith in Jesus Christ, a commitment to the Gospel message, and a profound understanding of their responsibility to transform the world. This interconnectedness, born out of shared experiences and nurtured by the exchange of knowledge and practices, laid the foundation for the Christian faith to flourish across continents and through the ages.

45. THE IMPACT OF EARLY CHRISTIANITY ON WESTERN CIVILIZATION

The impact of early Christianity on Western civilization is profound and undeniable. From its humble beginnings in the Roman Empire, Christianity spread rapidly, eventually becoming the dominant religion of the West, shaping its culture, institutions, and values in countless ways.

One of the most visible legacies of early Christianity is its influence on art and architecture. The magnificent cathedrals, churches, and monasteries that dot the European landscape are a testament to the faith's aesthetic vision. Art became a powerful vehicle for expressing and communicating Christian beliefs from the soaring arches and intricate stained-glass windows of Gothic cathedrals to the Byzantine mosaics and frescoes that adorned early Christian churches.

Early Christian art often depicted scenes from the Bible, saints' lives, and Jesus's teachings, inspiring artists and shaping artistic traditions for centuries. The development of religious iconography, with its symbolic language and imagery, deepened believers' understanding and devotion.

Christianity also had a profound impact on Western literature. The Bible, a collection of sacred texts, has inspired and influenced writers, poets, and thinkers throughout history. Its stories, characters, and themes have been interpreted and reinterpreted, influencing countless literary works.

Early Christian writers, such as Augustine of Hippo and Jerome, produced a vast corpus of theological treatises, philosophical writings, and devotional literature, shaping the intellectual landscape of the Western world. Their ideas and writings continued to be studied and debated in universities and monasteries, contributing to the development of scholarships and the transmission of knowledge.

In the realm of philosophy, early Christianity introduced new perspectives and challenged existing ideas. Early Church Fathers like Justin Martyr, Clement of Alexandria, and Origen sought to synthesize the Christian faith with Greek philosophical thought, leading to the development of Christian philosophy. They engaged in discussions about the nature of God, the soul, and the relationship between faith and reason, contributing to the ongoing dialogue between religion and philosophy.

Early Christianity's impact extended to the legal system as well. Christian values, such as compassion, forgiveness, and the sanctity of life, influenced the development of legal codes and the administration of justice. The emphasis on the equality of all people before God challenged traditional social hierarchies and contributed to the development of more inclusive and just legal systems.

Moreover, Christianity had a significant impact on social values. It promoted a new ethic of love, compassion, and service to the poor and needy. Early Christians established hospitals, orphanages, and other institutions to care for the sick, the vulnerable, and the marginalized. Jesus' teachings, particularly his emphasis on the Golden Rule, inspired acts of kindness and generosity, transforming social interactions and fostering a sense of community.

Early Christianity's influence on social values also extended to the family structure. The emphasis on marriage as a sacred union and the condemnation of divorce contributed to developing a more stable and enduring family unit. The church played a significant role in promoting the care and education of children and establishing schools and institutions to nurture future generations.

In conclusion, early Christianity's enduring legacy on Western civilization is vast and multifaceted. Its influence on art, literature, philosophy, law, and social values has shaped the West's cultural, intellectual, and spiritual landscape for centuries. From the majestic cathedrals to the profound works of literature, from the ethical frameworks of law to the values of compassion and service, early Christianity has left an indelible mark on Western society.

While the impact of early Christianity on the West is undeniable, it is also crucial to acknowledge the complexities and challenges accompanying its spread. From the Roman persecutions to the various controversies and conflicts within the church, early Christianity was not without its trials and tribulations. Yet, through these challenges, the faith grew stronger, its influence expanded, and its impact became increasingly profound.

As we move forward, it is essential to continue to study and understand the legacy of early Christianity, not only to appreciate its contributions but also to learn from its mistakes and to grapple with its ongoing relevance in a rapidly changing world. For the insights and values of early Christianity, while deeply rooted in its historical context, offer a timeless message that continues to resonate with people of all backgrounds and beliefs.

46. THE INFLUENCE OF EARLY CHRISTIANITY ON GLOBAL CULTURE

The influence of early Christianity on global culture is a vast and multifaceted story, one that continues to shape the world today. From its humble beginnings in the Roman Empire, Christianity spread like wildfire, weaving its way into the fabric of diverse societies and leaving an indelible mark on their values, beliefs, and traditions.

One of the most profound impacts of early Christianity was the establishment of a moral framework that transcended geographical boundaries and cultural differences. The teachings of Jesus, emphasizing love, compassion, forgiveness, and the inherent dignity of all people, resonated deeply with individuals across various walks of life. This ethical framework provided a unifying force, encouraging acts of kindness, promoting social justice, and challenging the inequalities in ancient societies. Christian communities established hospices for the sick, shelters for the poor, and schools for the disadvantaged, demonstrating a commitment to alleviating suffering and uplifting the marginalized.

The early Christians' dedication to education and the preservation of knowledge was another significant contribution to global culture. The establishment of monasteries and libraries, particularly in the West, played a crucial role in preserving ancient texts and transmitting knowledge across generations. This intellectual pursuit, fueled by a belief in the importance of understanding Scripture and engaging in theological discourse paved the way for the development of Christian theology, philosophy, and literature.

Christianity's influence extended beyond moral and intellectual spheres, shaping the very landscape of religious beliefs around the world. The conversion of emperors like Constantine in the 4th century AD marked a turning point, transforming Christianity from a persecuted religion to a dominant force within the Roman Empire. This shift profoundly affected the religious landscape, leading to the construction of magnificent churches, the establishment of religious institutions, and the integration Christian principles into law and governance. The spread of Christianity to diverse regions, from the British Isles to the Byzantine Empire, brought about significant cultural transformations, influencing art, architecture, music, and literature.

The impact of early Christianity on global culture is not without its complexities and controversies. The relationship between Christianity and political power, particularly in the centuries following the Roman Empire, has often been fraught with tension and conflict. The rise of religious intolerance and the use of faith to justify violence and oppression have marked some chapters in Christian history, raising critical questions about the true spirit of Christ's message and the responsibility of Christians to challenge injustice in all its forms actively.

Despite these challenges, the enduring legacy of early Christianity remains profound. Its emphasis on the fundamental equality and dignity of all people, its promotion of compassion and forgiveness, and its commitment to intellectual inquiry and the pursuit of justice continue to inspire individuals and communities across the globe. The principles of Christian faith have fueled movements for social reform, humanitarian action, and the pursuit of a more just and compassionate world.

Early Christianity's influence on global culture is a testament to the power of faith to transcend borders, cultures, and time. As we continue to grapple with the complexities of our interconnected world, understanding the origins and evolution of Christianity offers valuable insights into the forces that have shaped our shared history and continue to influence our present and future. From the teachings of Jesus to the practices of early Christian communities, the legacy of early Christianity serves as a powerful reminder of the potential for faith to inspire hope, promote understanding, and guide us toward a more humane and just world.

47. THE ONGOING RELEVANCE OF EARLY CHRISTIAN THOUGHT

The echoes of early Christian thought continue to resonate in the modern world, offering profound insights into the human experience and the enduring search for meaning. The early Christians grappled with questions about human nature, the nature of God, and the purpose of life, their struggles and triumphs echoing through centuries to inform our understanding. Their reflections on the nature of sin and redemption, the power of forgiveness, and the importance of love remain deeply relevant, offering guidance and inspiration in navigating the complexities of our own lives.

One of the most profound legacies of early Christianity lies in its articulation of the inherent dignity and value of every human being. The early Christians, inspired by the life and teachings of Jesus, rejected the hierarchical social structures of their time and embraced a radical message of equality. They saw a reflection of the divine image in every person, regardless of their social standing. This revolutionary concept challenged the social norms of their day, challenging the accepted hierarchies and fostering a spirit of compassion and social justice.

The early Christians' emphasis on love and compassion continues to be a powerful force for good in the world. Their teachings on forgiveness, self-sacrifice, and the love of one's neighbor have shaped countless charitable organizations, humanitarian movements, and acts of kindness throughout history. The Gospel message of love, embodied in the life of Jesus, continues to inspire individuals and communities to reach out to those in need and to strive for a more just and compassionate world.

Early Christian thought also offers profound insights into the nature of spirituality. The early Christians sought to live a life transformed by their faith, seeking to align their thoughts, words, and actions with the teachings of Jesus. They emphasized the importance of prayer, meditation, and cultivating a deep inner life. Their writings on spiritual disciplines like asceticism, contemplation, and the practice of virtues offer valuable tools for navigating the challenges of modern life and cultivating a more meaningful and purposeful existence.

The early Christians grappled with the complexities of human nature, recognizing both the capacity for good and the tendency toward evil. They wrestled with the nature of sin and its consequences, seeking to understand how human beings can overcome their limitations and achieve a closer relationship with God. Their writings on repentance, forgiveness, and the transformative power of grace provide timeless insights into the human condition, offering hope and redemption amidst life's challenges.

The enduring relevance of early Christian thought is a testament to its intellectual and spiritual insights. Its ongoing influence on art, literature, music, and culture, from the soaring cathedrals of the Middle Ages to the vibrant paintings of the Renaissance, from the powerful hymns of the Church to the enduring literature of faith, has profoundly shaped the artistic and cultural landscape of the Western world. It inspires creative expressions of faith, reminding us of the enduring power of human imagination and the beauty of the human spirit.

In a world struggling with complex social, political, and environmental challenges, the insights of early Christian beliefs offer a beacon of hope and inspiration. Their teachings on love, compassion, forgiveness, and the pursuit of a just and compassionate world continue to challenge us to live with integrity, to seek justice for the marginalized, and to strive for a more harmonious and sustainable future. Their emphasis on spiritual growth and the cultivation of a deep inner life provides a path toward more significant meaning and purpose amidst the complexities of modern life.

The legacy of early Christianity is a testament to the enduring power of faith, hope, and love. The insights and teachings of the early Christians continue to resonate with us today, offering timeless wisdom and a compass for navigating life's challenges. As we delve into the history of the early church, we not only gain a deeper understanding of the origins of Christianity but also encounter a rich tapestry of human experience, spiritual seeking, and enduring hope.

48. THE CHALLENGES AND OPPORTUNITIES FACING CHRISTIANITY TODAY

The 21st century presents Christianity with unique challenges and opportunities. Globalization, secularism, and a diverse religious landscape have significantly shaped the Christian experience, leading believers to confront new questions and navigate an increasingly complex world. These challenges and opportunities call for a thoughtful and engaged response from the Christian community.

One of the most significant challenges is the rise of Secularism, which has led to a decline in traditional religious practices and a growing skepticism toward religious claims. In many parts of the world, Christianity is no longer the dominant cultural force it once was. Secular values and ideologies often clash with Christian teachings, leading to debates on issues like same-sex marriage, abortion, and the role of religion in public life. These conflicts can create a sense of alienation for Christians, who may feel marginalized or misunderstood in a society that increasingly embraces a secular worldview.

However, this challenge also allows Christians to re-engage with the world meaningfully.

By offering a compelling message of hope, love, and compassion, Christians can bridge the gap between faith and secular society. They can engage in dialogue with those with different viewpoints, seeking common ground and promoting understanding. This requires a willingness to listen, learn, and respond to the concerns of those not traditionally religious, demonstrating the relevance and value of Christian faith in a modern context.

Globalization has also had a profound impact on Christianity. With the increasing interconnectedness of nations and cultures, Christians encounter a more comprehensive range of religious perspectives and cultural practices than ever before. This exposure to diverse faiths can enrich Christian understanding of the world, leading to a more profound appreciation for other religious traditions and a more nuanced view of religious pluralism.

However, globalization also presents challenges, as Christians deal with the tensions between their faith and the values of diverse cultures. The integration of global economies and the spread of secular ideologies can also lead to the erosion of traditional Christian values in some communities. Christians are called to navigate these challenges with wisdom, seeking to uphold their convictions while engaging with the world respectfully and constructively.

Furthermore, the diversity of religious perspectives in a globalized world creates opportunities and challenges for Christian missions. While Christianity has historically been a missionary faith, seeking to share its message with the world, the current landscape requires a more nuanced approach. Christians must engage in dialogue with other faiths, seeking common ground and understanding while remaining faithful to their beliefs. This approach emphasizes dialogue over proselytism.

The challenge of engaging with diverse religious perspectives is also an opportunity for Christians to learn from other faiths. By engaging in respectful dialogue, Christians can broaden their understanding of the human experience, deepen their appreciation for different worldviews, and discover new insights into the nature of faith. This open-minded approach can enrich Christian theology and practice, leading to a more nuanced and compassionate understanding of the world.

In conclusion, the challenges and opportunities facing Christianity today are inextricably linked to the forces of globalization, secularism, and religious pluralism. The decline of traditional religious practices and the rise of secular values are significant challenges Christianity faces. These changes in societal norms are reshaping the landscape for Christians striving to maintain their faith in a rapidly changing world. Secular values create a unique set of challenges for Christians seeking to preserve their faith in a changing world. However, these challenges also present opportunities for renewal and growth. By re-engaging with the world meaningfully, promoting dialogue and understanding, and embracing a more nuanced approach to mission, Christians can demonstrate the relevance and value of their faith in a complex and diverse world.

The enduring legacy of early Christianity provides invaluable insights for navigating these challenges. The early church faced persecution, theological controversies, and cultural clashes, yet it thrived and spread its message across the Roman Empire and beyond. Studying the early Christians' experiences can guide contemporary believers, providing examples of resilience, faith, and the power of the Gospel message in diverse contexts.

By drawing upon the strength and wisdom of the early church, Christians today can embrace the challenges and opportunities of the 21st century with hope and conviction. Through engagement with the world, dialogue with diverse perspectives, and a renewed focus on the core values of faith, love, and compassion, Christianity can continue to offer a message of hope and renewal for future generations.

The Future of Christianity and the Legacy of its Beginnings

The study of the early church reveals a potent blend of resilience, innovation, and faith that has shaped the trajectory of Christianity for centuries. As we look to the future of Christianity, we find that its beginnings provide a rich wellspring of insights that remain profoundly relevant to contemporary Christian life and society.

Despite its nascent status, the early church engaged in complex theological debates, navigating internal disputes and evolving beliefs. This dynamic process of scrutinizing faith and challenging doctrines remains essential for the health of any religion. Through their councils and engagement with Scripture, the early Christians modeled a tradition of ongoing dialogue and intellectual inquiry that is crucial in the modern era. The challenges of cultural pluralism, scientific advancements, and evolving moral landscapes necessitate Christian communities to engage in respectful dialogue and critical reflection on their beliefs considering the changing world.

Secondly, the early Christians' commitment to community and service is a beacon of hope for contemporary society. The early church prioritized the poor, the sick, and the marginalized, establishing a model of caring for the most vulnerable. This commitment to social needs and alleviating suffering, deeply rooted in Jesus' teachings, stands as a potent reminder of Christians' moral obligation to address the inequities of our world actively. From addressing issues like poverty, hunger, and racial discrimination to advocating for human rights, Christians today can draw inspiration from the early church's dedication to living out their faith in tangible ways that touch the lives of others.

Thirdly, the early Christians' unwavering courage in the face of persecution offers a potent reminder of the power of faith to sustain individuals and communities in difficult times. They endured imprisonment, exile, and martyrdom, demonstrating the enduring power of faith even in the face of immense hardship.

In an era marked by political turmoil, social unrest, and cultural clashes, Christians today can find strength and resilience in the stories of early believers who remained steadfast in their convictions despite adversity. Their example serves as a testament to the power of faith to provide hope, solace, and strength amidst trials, urging contemporary Christians to stand up for their beliefs, even when faced with opposition and challenges.

However, the future of Christianity has its challenges. The secularization of many Western societies, the rise of alternative belief systems, and the fragmentation of Christian communities pose significant obstacles to the propagation of the faith. The current era demands that Christians engage in a dialogue with secular perspectives, actively address the concerns of a skeptical society, and build bridges with other religious traditions. In this context, the early church's approach to interfaith dialogue and its ability to adapt its message to diverse cultures offers a model for contemporary Christians. Despite its challenges, the early church proved adaptable and innovative, forging connections with diverse cultures, languages, and social spheres. This flexibility and open-mindedness are essential for Christianity to thrive in the globalized, interconnected world of the 21st century. Looking ahead, Christianity's future hinges on its ability to learn from its past, remain committed to its core values, and actively engage in the world.

The early church's story is a testament to the enduring power of faith, the significance of community, and the importance of resilience in the face of challenges. As Christians today navigate the complexities of the modern world, they can draw inspiration from the early church's legacy, embracing its lessons to forge a vibrant and impactful future for the faith. The early church's story is not merely a relic of history; it is a powerful narrative that continues to shape the trajectory of Christianity and offers a compelling vision for its future.

ACKNOWLEDGMENTS

I would also like to express my sincere gratitude to my family and friends for their unwavering support and understanding during the demanding stages of writing this book. Their encouragement and patience helped me stay focused and motivated.

I am especially indebted to the Sunday Night Bible Study I facilitate. It causes me to stay focused and dive deep into the word of God each week.

Finally, I am grateful to the readers who will engage in this work. I hope this book will serve as a valuable resource for scholars, students, and anyone seeking to deepen their understanding of the origins and enduring impact of Christianity.

I always wish to help others become closer to Christ and the Word of God. If you have any questions or would like to receive a free digital copy of the bible, please email me:

Michael@thesalubriousgroup.com

GLOSSARY

Apostolic Succession:
The belief that the apostles' authority was passed down to bishops and their successors.

Canon:
The official list of books accepted as scripture in a particular religious tradition.

Christology:
The study of the person and work of Jesus Christ.

Gnosticism:
A group of ancient religious movements that emphasized secret knowledge and a dualistic view of the world.

Heresy:
This belief is considered to be contrary to the teachings of the church.

Monasticism:
A way of life characterized by a commitment to prayer, contemplation, and service, often lived in a communal setting.

Trinity:
The doctrine is that God exists in three persons: Father, Son, and Holy Spirit.

ABOUT THE AUTHOR

Michael Lee lives in Central Texas on a small farm he and his wife Laura manage. This is the same lifestyle he grew up in Southeast Oklahoma. Introduced to strict Baptist teaching, he was taught that the pastor was always correct. While enrolled in Hillsdale Free Will Baptist College, aka Randall University, and doing deep research in scripture, he discovered that was only sometimes true. For the next fifty years, Michael attended every church and denomination available. Only in recent years, and the advent of the internet, did he realize the abundance of information available to us.

Michael is passionate about sharing the gospel and biblical history to prove and establish the validity of scripture. This is the first of several books in a series of factual Bible studies.

Made in the USA
Columbia, SC
03 December 2024

47235045R00102